# Endorsements

*Dr. Nick Eno has a way of first illuminating and then healing the traumas that come from having your spirit scarred by rejection and abandonment.*

*In his new ground-breaking book,* The Orphan Syndrome, *Dr. Eno lovingly walks us into his spiritual surgical suite and deftly does the spiritual and psychological surgery needed to remove the soulical cancers and then allows us to walk home—free.*

—**Chris Hill**
Senior Pastor
The Potter's House of Denver

*Dr. Nick Eno's latest book,* The Orphan Syndrome: Breaking Free and Finding Home, *helps us to identify times and/or ways of woundedness in our lives that led to a wounded spirit. Through the various illustrations as well as his personal disclosure, we see how the enemy of our soul uses circumstances to hinder us from "breaking free and finding home." In this phenomenal work, Dr. Eno shows us that we can actually become free in the Presence of our loving Father and through Christ Jesus be empowered to live lives of victory! Whether for you or someone you are helping, this book is an inspirational tool serving as an agent of healing and wholeness. It causes us to seek after the love of God choosing to allow ourselves to flow in the fruit of His Holy Spirit no longer giving opportunity to the orphan spirit.*

—**Rosalind Caldwell Stanley**
Author and Lead Pastoral Counselor and Trainer
Because of Grace Christian Training Center

*Dr. Eno has exposed a sensitive nerve in the hindered growth of emotional intelligence. The orphan syndrome is a little known experienced phenomenon I have found present in thousands of adult prisoners I have worked with for over 30 years. America's prisons are filled with men and women who were raised by their grandparents or by the state as a result of one or both biological parents abandoning them physically and/or emotionally. The Orphan Syndrome should be placed in every prison in America as a psychological treatment tool. It is a great book!*

—**Paul Carlin, Ph.D., LBT**
The Ministry Church, Inc.

*Nick Eno has written an important book about experiencing the love of God. So many go through life feeling disconnected, unloved, alone. But isolation is a lie. The tragic irony is that we live in a world that has the glorious community of the Trinity at its center. We exist in an ocean of love. Nick writes out of his own experience with unspeakable pain and his professional experience in helping others. He can help you break free and find home with a family, the Holy Trinity, which will never leave.*

—**Gary W. Moon, M.Div., Ph.D.**
Executive Director
Martin Institute and Dallas Willard Center
Westmont College
Author, *Apprenticeship with Jesus*

When I recently read The Orphan Syndrome, I was shocked that I had this syndrome, as do MANY of the people I know, even though we were all raised by our biological parents until that day when we left home after high school. In this book, Dr. Nick Eno has unearthed, for me, critically important issues which have been buried within me for decades. And Dr. Eno artfully guides his readers through an emotional healing and spiritual healing journey which he has discovered to heal wounds in his own life as well as countless patients that he has counseled.

As a board-certified internist and cardiologist, over the years, I have come to recognize that unhealed emotional or spiritual wounds often result in physical disease as well and that the physical disease cannot be fully healed until the causative emotional and spiritual wounds are healed. I strongly believe that every healthcare practitioner should read The Orphan Syndrome and recommend that their patients read it as well.

Even if you are not an orphan yourself according to Dr. Eno's definition, you almost certainly know several such orphans who could benefit tremendously from reading this book.

—**W. Lee Cowden, MD, MD(H)**
Chairman of the Scientific Advisory Board
Academy of Comprehensive Integrative Medicine

The people whose lives will be radically changed by this book are orphans—and we are all orphans. With penetrating insight, Dr. Nick Eno explains what the orphan syndrome is, how all of us can shed that life-quenching belief, and how we can be embraced by the Spirit of adoption that will change the way we live in every moment.

—**James L. Rubart**
Bestselling author of The Five Times I Met Myself

*I've been wanting to write to you because your book has woken up so many thoughts and emotions. It is truly an amazing book and so filled with wise thoughts that I can only read a few pages at a time. Your book is having a profound effect on me. I've known all along that being bitter or sad isn't helping me or the people around me, but I hadn't found a way to get over these feelings. I was doing the good deeds, helping and healing others, but I've indeed been an orphan myself. So thank you Nick, the book isn't even halfway through but it has already helped me and opened my eyes. I can't wait to continue it and let new revelations and deep feelings come.*

—MarjoValonen, MD
Helsinki, Finland

# THE
# ORPHAN
# SYNDROME

# THE ORPHAN SYNDROME

### BREAKING FREE *and* FINDING HOME

## Dr. Nick Eno

REDEMPTION PRESS

Published by Redemption Press, PO Box 427, Enumclaw, WA 98022
Toll Free (844) 2REDEEM (273-3336)

Redemption Press is honored to present this title in partnership with the author. The views expressed or implied in this work are those of the author. Redemption Press provides our imprint seal representing design excellence, creative content and high quality production.

Scriptures marked KJV are taken from the *King James Version* (KJV): *King James Version*, public domain.

Scriptures marked NCV are taken from the *New Century Version* (NCV): Scripture taken from the *New Century Version*®. Copyright© 2005 by Thomas Nelson, Inc. Used by permission. All rights reserved.

Scriptures marked NIV are taken from the *New International Version* (NIV): Scripture taken from *The Holy Bible, New International Version*®. Copyright© 1973, 1978, 1984, 2011 by Biblica, Inc.™ Used by permission of Zondervan.

Scriptures marked NKJV are taken from the *New King James Version* (NKJV): Scripture taken from the *New King James Version*®. Copyright© 1982 by Thomas Nelson, Inc. Used by permission. All rights reserved.

Scripture quotations marked (NLT) are taken from the *Holy Bible, New Living Translation,* copyright © 1996. Used by permission of Tyndale House Publishers Inc., Wheaton, IL 60189 USA. All rights reserved.

Some names of individuals used are fictitious. While the stories of individuals are real, relevant facts have been changed to protect client identities and some composites have been used

ISBN 13: 978-1-63232-647-8 (SC)
         978-1-63232-648-5 (HC)
         978-1-63232-653-9 (ePub)
         978-1-63232-654-6 (Mobi)

Library of Congress Catalog Card Number: 2015959260

*Dedicated to my mother, Felicia Mambo Eno.*
*I send you love always*

# Contents

# Acknowledgments

This book is the fruit of God's love shown to me by many people in countless ways.

Thanks to Dave and Deborah Durrett, Michael and Debbie Rasa, Tom and Nancy Cooper, Kent and Bennett Vandiver, and Janet Duhon for your support and encouragement.

Thanks to Athena Dean Holtz for helping me see the potential of this work, Inger Logelin, my conscientious and meticulous editor, and the rest of the staff at Redemption Press.

Thanks to Christy Davis and Natacha Byrams for your valuable input.

I am indebted to Pamela, Nicole, Elwynn, and Dreamy for your encouragement, patience, and abiding love.

*Soli Deo Gloria!*

# Foreword

Each and every one of us is brought into this world alone. Yes, we may have parents who raise us, and some of us don't. The constant is we each enter and exit this world alone, a worldly orphan. This is not how it is meant to be. God, our Heavenly Daddy, is with us from conception to departure. No one is an orphan, spiritually, except by choice.

In Nick Eno's book, life examples are given, personalities and struggles are discussed, and conclusions made about the root causes of every example. There is hope for every orphan spirit through the healing power of Jesus Christ and the grace that is freely offered to each one of us, a gift from God our heavenly Father.

My prayer is those seeking peace will find it through faith and through grace. The answers to earth's questions are found in grace; the acceptance of grace will heal an orphan spirit.

—**David J. Durrett**
CEO
New Birmingham Inc.

# Introduction

She sat across from me, her face buried in her hands, as she sobbed. "I am so tired, so dry inside." Heather, forty-nine, a mother of two grown children, had just opened up about the gnawing loneliness and despair that had been her constant companions since she was seven. She felt disconnected from her children and unloved by her husband.

Heather had professed Christ when she was nine, but had never experienced the kind of personal relationship that others often describe. Heather worked really hard to dot the i's and cross the t's in her life—college degree, married with children by twenty-five, a very successful career in real estate, and active in her church and community. Yet there she sat in my office—fearful, lonely, depressed, on the verge of divorce, in constant physical pain, and feeling very alienated from God and her family.

*She feels like an orphan.* Heather has an orphan spirit. The different manifestations of that grave condition constitute the orphan syndrome.

In my twenty-five years of counseling, similar scenarios have been replayed over and over with different people of all ages. I write this book to help all those whose hearts feel orphaned like Heather.

There is no shortcut to Christian maturity. It takes time as well as our cooperation. It is a process, not an event. Too often we want God to deliver us by miracles. However, God wants to develop our character so we can apply his principles, and not end up in the graves that we dig for ourselves.

Thomas Aquinas wrote:

> Two things are required in order to attain eternal life: the grace of God and man's will. And although God has made man without man's help, He does not sanctify him without his cooperation.[1]

Over the long history of the church, different groups have proffered various formulaic and quick fixes to achieve union with Christ. The hype typically did not match the result. Today is no different.

Wilderness excursions, weekend intensives, deliverance sessions, ubiquitous conferences, breaking soul/generational ties, and self-help psycho-babblers are still offering people silver bullets that consistently fail to assuage man's greatest need—*love*!

Our deepest anxiety stems from the fear of losing love—feeling isolated and without comfort in a cold, evil world. We know, deep down, we were not created to be orphans, yet "sonship" eludes most of us.

As Jesus prepared to depart this world, he comforted his followers with these words, "I will not leave you alone, like orphans. I will come back for you" (John 14:18 NCV). He promised to send the Comforter, the *Paraclete*, to lead his followers into all truth.

Yet, today too many professing Christians feel isolated and burdened by the constant pressure to perform for acceptance. They are exhausted from feeding off the trough of stale mantras, rote worship and shallow fellowship. Self-help sermons, no matter how titillating or affirming, lack the power to touch us in our "inward parts" (Ps. 55:6).

We crave to be loved and to love back.

Our rituals and liturgies are directed mostly at external cues. Thus the cycle of eruption leads to doubling down which leads to frustration, which leads to greater doubling down, which leads to more eruption, which leads to exhaustion, and continues to be perpetrated. We have drunk deep from the wells of faith but ignored what makes faith work—*love* (see Gal. 5:6).

## Cycle of Eruption

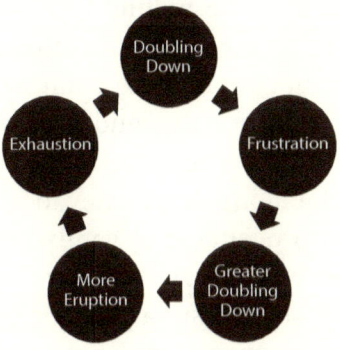

This cycle produces "the weary saint," seemingly the norm these days. We soldier on like orphans without a father. We work hard to hide our deep hurts from each other, cope by escaping through consumerism and hedonism, and medicate our dread of the future with "Big Pharma."

After twenty-five years of counseling in the "basement" with the saints, I have sadly come to the conclusion that the kind of deep inner transformation believers crave is largely missing in today's iteration of church. We are trained to confront sin by reframing it in the context of cheap grace, blaming the devil, or toughening our resolve to conquer sin through the force of our own will.

The kind of self-examination (1 Cor. 11:28) that is required to help us identify and own our deep alienation from love (God) is typically reserved for the few minutes before sporadic communion services. Surrender is not an option—strive on Christian soldier! "Strive on" could be a fitting anthem.

*The Orphan Syndrome: Breaking Free and Finding Home* seeks to help us identify the source of our deepest wounds, describe their effects, and offer us practical and time-tested ways to offer the deepest parts of ourselves to Christ. Only God can transform our crushed spirits and broken hearts into healing altars. His love alone transforms us from orphans into sons and daughters.

However, we must be willing to cultivate habits and virtues that prime us for such inner change. These habits include, but are not limited to, confession, repentance, solitude, worship, simplicity, and a lifestyle of sacrifice and generosity. Often we need the help of an anointed and qualified counselor along the journey to freedom in Christ.

As Theresa of Lysieux so elegantly stated, "If you are willing to serenely bear the trial of being displeasing to yourself, then you will be for Jesus a pleasant place of shelter."[2]

As you read these pages, my prayer is that you choose to surrender your deepest hurts to God and allow his love to penetrate and abide in your heart. That way you can become a vital part of the healing community that fulfills Jesus' test of true discipleship.

> Your love for one another will prove to the world that you are my disciples.
>
> (John 13:35 NLT)

# A Picture of the
# Wounded Spirit

It was a crisp February morning in Dallas, Texas. I was at home resting after an intense weekend of ministry when the phone rang. It was a dear friend—an associate pastor at a very prominent ministry in the Dallas area, bearing news a friend never wants to hear.

"Nick, Jay shot himself this morning." He had been found by one of his children.

Horrified and in disbelief, reeling, and pondering numerous questions, I listened as my friend filled me in on the details, including the funeral arrangements for Jay. This did not make sense. I was well acquainted with this family, especially his wife, Janet. The couple appeared to be the very pillars of stability and Christian maturity. Long-term members of a well-established church, they were involved in the highest levels of ministry.

I drove out to the family's home that evening and attended the wake the next day. At the committal service, Jay's pastor from his hometown spoke first. He assured everyone that Jay was definitely born again with a sure testimony, and then proceeded to describe his firsthand account of Jay's experience with the baptism of the Holy Ghost.

Jay was driving, and the pastor was talking to him about the Holy Spirit's baptism. After speaking about the baptism with fire, the pastor invited Jay to ask God for the gift. Well, boy did he receive it! Jay began speaking in tongues, and drove for several miles with his eyes closed without crashing! Sitting in the passenger's seat, the pastor admitted he was terrified, yet rejuvenated by the experience. The questions on my mind were amplified. This man was saved, sanctified, and filled with the Holy Spirit! How could he shoot himself?

Next, a striking young preacher was invited to speak. The tall, blonde, and muscular young man tried to speak, but sobbed bitterly. All he could mutter was, "Please forgive me, Lord. Please forgive me!" Finally, composing himself, he proceeded to describe his relationship with Jay over the previous eighteen months. Jay had taken a liking to him and the two would have breakfast every Thursday morning together and talk about faith and life in general. They had just met as usual, the previous Thursday before this tragedy. Something seemed different about that last meeting, though. Unlike in previous meetings, Jay wanted reassurance that his family, especially his wife and friends, loved him.

The young man broke down again as he went on to say the Lord woke him up that Thursday morning and impressed upon his heart to fast and pray for Jay to be healed of a *wounded spirit*. He felt no sense of urgency at the time, so he rolled over and decided to put it off until the following week.

"Oh, Lord, forgive me," he wailed.

Feeling his pain, I began weeping too. First for Jay, then his family; then I wept for my own compassion deficits; and finally for the body of Christ.

Jay had seemingly crossed all the "t's" and dotted the "i's" required by full-gospel Christianity to ensure a victorious life, even until the end. Yet, on a Sunday morning, alone and in despair, he took his own life.

The service came to an end, and we followed the flag-draped casket of this pastor and veteran to the Dallas/Fort Worth National Cemetery.

## An All-Too-Familiar Fight

After saying goodbye to Jay's family, I approached the broken young preacher who had been meeting with Jay and invited him to breakfast. We agreed to meet the following Thursday at a diner midpoint from our homes.

During breakfast, he proceeded to elaborate on what had transpired at Jay's funeral. He had woken up early that fateful Thursday with an urgent impression upon his heart to fast and pray for Jay. After inquiring further of the Lord, he discerned he needed to fast and pray so Jay would be healed of a *wounded spirit*.

"Wounded spirit! What is that? And how do you diagnose it?" I desperately asked.

I had been a licensed counselor by then for two decades. I was in clinical practice, served as head of counseling for a large church, and had spent over ten years in full-time ministry—yet this was a relatively new concept to me.

Weren't salvation and sanctification supposed to take care of all those things? After all, the Bible categorically states, "Therefore, if anyone is in Christ, he is a new creation; old things have passed away; behold, all things have become new" (2 Cor. 5:17 NKJV).

As I spent some time with Jay's widow, Janet, and probed further into this issue, Jay's tragic end started to make sense to me.

I asked Janet, "When was Jay happiest in your marriage?"

Her response was heart piercing. "Once when he was in Korea, and the other time when he was in Vietnam."

Jay had resisted his wife's love and the love of his children for over five decades! Even more devastating, Jay had resisted God's love all his life. He would give the shirt off his back to help a stranger. He gave of himself and his substance to the service of the Lord. However, in his personal relationships, he felt unworthy of love. He would deflect and deny love at every turn. He always felt detached, unwanted, fearful, ashamed, and was without joy.

Cases like this one have become increasingly prevalent. Preachers, ministers, and Christians in general who have a covenant with the source of life—our Abba Father—find themselves empty, distraught, and overwhelmed with despair, as they battle bouts of depression while in God's service.

Something is wrong with this picture.

Jay's funeral began my search to understand what I now refer to as the *orphan syndrome*.

On another evening, not long after this tragic event, I read a local paper, with the headline:

MACON GA PREACHER FATALLY SHOOTS SELF BETWEEN SUNDAY SERVICES.
The pastor of a church in Macon, Georgia apparently shot himself fatally after returning to his home from Sunday services, authorities said. The Rev. Teddy Parker Jr., pastor of Bibb Mt. Zion Baptist Church was found dead

in the driveway of his home . . . he was 42. He was found by his wife. Authorities believe the gunshot wound that caused his death was self-inflicted. The couple has two daughters . . . It could not be determined if they were with their mother when she found him. . . . News of his death sent shockwaves through religious circles.[3]

Yet another case of the orphan syndrome.
I was determined to find answers.

## My Own Wounds

My quest to learn more led me to Conway, South Carolina to a conference on "Experiencing the Father's Embrace." There on the altar of ministry, I had to confront my own "orphan" state, born out of a wounded spirit. I vividly remember the events that shifted my entire paradigm on belonging, and my ability to connect to God and others.

One night in my early teens, I heard a lot of commotion, then loud voices, and finally footsteps running toward my bedroom door. Suddenly the door swung open and my mother rushed in with my father in hot pursuit. She dashed in, slammed the door shut behind her, and then locked the bolt from the inside. In short order, my father was banging on the door on the outside, commanding me, "Open the door!" My mom was leaning against the door on the inside begging me, "Don't let him in."

I can still feel the deep sense of angst and confusion that paralyzed me. I felt like an accordion—pulled wide from both sides, then released. I bit my fingernails until they bled as I heard my siblings crying outside the door.

My mother eventually left that night, reassuring us, "I'll be back in a few days." She never returned.

Fast forward to July 3, 2003. I had just dropped my wife of fifteen years off at the airport. She was ostensibly going to visit her mother in New Jersey. Her father had died a few months earlier, so this was a planned visit. I returned home, to find she had left a note from her lover informing me she was not coming back. I agonized over how to break the news to my ten-year-old daughter, only to find out her mother had told her she was leaving, and had sworn her to silence a full day before she left.

I have never felt as hurt and betrayed as that before or since.

Being emotionally hurt is not all that resulted from these two instances of rejection. I was spiritually wounded. My spirit, the core of who I am, was wounded and therefore, dysfunctional. All that flowed out of me was tainted by these traumatic events. As Proverbs 18:14 (NIV) explains: "The spirit of a man will sustain him in sickness but a wounded spirit who can bear?"

That day at the conference was a turning point in my spiritual restoration, a milestone in my spiritual development, and a moment of revelation on how a wounded spirit produces the orphan syndrome. From that day on, I began the journey toward *sonship*.

I believe Jay's outcome would have been different if someone could have ministered to his wounded spirit. The orphan syndrome would have never been produced in him, and this man of God's life could have been preserved.

The message of the *Orphan Syndrome* is to preserve you, and help you heal. It is real help for real hurt. Whether you are in the depths of despair and flirting with thoughts of suicide, or simply feeling cold and empty, our Heavenly

Father—the source of life—is pursuing you to bring you to wholeness.

The following chapters will help you identify symptoms of a wounded spirit and how it leads to an orphan syndrome—and how to heal. I believe the word of the Lord when it says, "Surely goodness and mercy shall follow me, all the days of my life" (Ps. 23:6 KJV).

# The Expression of an Unhealthy Spirit

He leaned back on the sofa, fingers locked tightly behind his head. "Last year I preached one hundred and thirty sermons at my home church."

"Wow!" I responded.

"It gets better," he replied. "I spoke over a hundred times in conferences in the US and fifty times overseas. I preached to over 400,000 people in person, and reached over fifty million people worldwide via our television ministry."

Then he looked down and admitted, "I know deep down I need to slow down, but I just don't know how. I keep thinking . . ." his voice trailed off wistfully.

"Thinking about what?" I asked.

"Nothing. I just have to do it for now."

My heart sank as tears welled up in my eyes. Despite the outward trappings of success, I could feel the depth of the weariness in his soul. The picture that flashed through my mind was of a man riding a tiger and being deathly afraid to dismount.

My pastor friend went on to describe the tremendous responsibility he felt toward God and all the people who depended on him. Souls needed to get saved and be discipled. The staff needed to be paid. His wife and kids, as well as an ever-increasing number of extended family members, all needed to be taken care of.

He just could not see an exit ramp at that point. He tried to take a few days off every month, but he was overwhelmed by guilt every time he went away to rest. He said, "I'm starting to feel trapped." This fueled anger in him, and even rage, toward God and people. At that point he was questioning not just the love of God, but his very existence.

The signal trait of the orphan syndrome is this inability to find rest. There is no Sabbath. The individual feels compelled to be "on" all the time. Rest requires laying down our "tools," trusting the world will not fall apart while we are disengaged. A lack of basic trust is the cardinal characteristic of a crushed or wounded spirit (see Ps. 131).

I peered into the packed waiting room through the glass partition. I observed an elderly couple with their adult child sitting between them. The anguish and sadness on their faces was palpable. On the other side of the room, a young mother was trying to reign in her listless toddler. Across from me, a middle-aged gentleman's face was buried in the pages of a fat novel, an escape from all the pain around him.

A feeling of deep compassion tinged with mild resignation washed over me. Oh, the human condition!

And then I saw her. Dressed in bold colors, she was wearing a hat that had a lot going on upon it. I opened the door and approached her. "Julie? Hi, I'm Nick, your counselor." I led her down the hallway into my office and she settled into a sofa facing the door.

"I see you were referred to me by your pastor."

"Yes, indeed."

We then engaged in small talk about her church, the outreach ministries and some mutual acquaintances.

"Welcome again. What's hurting?"

"Well, I guess I wore my pastor out so he sent me to you," Julie retorted with a smirk.

I nodded in her direction letting a pregnant pause stand.

"This is something I have been struggling with for the longest time. Seems like I'm the only one asking the hard questions. I don't know if people are afraid or what?"

"What? Afraid of who?"

"Well, it's a long story."

Julie then proceeded to relay a family tragedy that happened when she was just nine years old. Her father, her precious daddy whom she adored, was savagely murdered by two intruders. He was stabbed several times and then bludgeoned almost beyond recognition. The assailants then set their home on fire. Thankfully, Julie was out of town with her mother on that fateful day.

Now well into her forties, it was clear to me she was still reliving that defining trauma as if it had just happened. Her tears, her despair, and her clenched fist all displayed a soul in perpetual mourning.

"My God! That's awful," I gasped as I peered at her through my tear-misted reading glasses.

"So tell me, where was God? Why? Why? Why? My daddy was such a good man, a godly man, a praying man," she sobbed.

I grabbed a box of tissue and gently set it next to her.

"He was an angel. He helped everyone in the neighborhood. I remember hearing him praying, sometimes all night."

"Wow, so sorry," I muttered.

She finally composed herself, took a deep breath and dabbed her cheeks. She then leaned back, folded her arms tightly and stared at me. "So, do you believe God is sovereign?" she asked.

"Well, yeah," I replied.

"Do you believe he is good?"

"Um, yeah," I replied.

"So, help me understand. He is in control, right? So how can he let such evil happen and still be good?"

"Uh . . ." I began to explain, but she interrupted me.

"And please don't tell me about man's will and all that jazz," she spat out.

Julie then began to rant about the cowardly "so-called Christians" like her mom, who drink the "Kool-Aid" about God's goodness, in spite of the evidence to the contrary. To her, God was either bad or impotent. Her quest for the truth was her stated main purpose in life. It was so all-consuming she didn't have time, nor the desire for, marriage or family.

With our time winding down, I finally got a word in. "I honestly do not know why you came to see me. It looks like your mind is pretty well made up."

She shrugged and then stood up.

"Well, I promised my pastor I would reach out to you. I am a woman of my word."

I found out later that Julie scheduled another appointment with me and then cancelled it.

Julie personifies another devastating aspect of the orphan syndrome. That is, the unwillingness to reframe and process deep hurt. She practices the presence of her trauma. It looms so large in the present that it drowns out her past and it eclipses her future. It alienates her from God and man. Imagine the loneliness, hopelessness, and anguish of a soul full of questions, but unwilling to accept any answer that does not agree with her stance.

In Julie's world, God must be second—the same stance Lucifer took when he wanted God's place—a lonely place to be indeed.

Gwendolyn is a middle-aged professional woman, a nursing supervisor at a well-known hospital. She is assertive, confident, and easy to get along with—on the job. However, at home, it is a different matter. Married twenty years to Donald, the couple has two grown children, Don Jr., 27 and Lisa, 25.

Both children dropped out of college, are living at home and have no jobs. Donald has not had a steady job for the past twenty-five years. He has gotten involved with all kinds of "get-rich-quick" schemes, losing large sums of money along the way. Every time there is a financial crisis, he'll get a job—furniture or insurance salesman, or stocker at the grocery store, but would quit after a few weeks because he could not get along with the other employees.

Don Jr. is a talented artist, but feels his true calling is stand-up comedy. He does not feel the need to put himself out there, and is plying his craft until he is discovered. He is content lazing around the house griping about how much his mom enables his dad.

Lisa quit college and eloped with the first man she ever dated. The relationship was a disaster from the beginning, costing the family thousands of dollars to get her out of a

Mexican jail. She's currently at home, sleeps all day and is out partying all night.

Gwendolyn feels responsible for all of these people. Recently, she started having panic attacks at work. Her confidence is starting to sag so she made an appointment to see me.

"Could you describe a typical day for you?" I asked her.

"Well, I get up before dawn and fix breakfast for Don and the kids, set the warmers and leave for work about 6:30 a.m. It takes about forty-five minutes to get to work."

"Okay."

"If no emergencies, I usually get back home about 6:00 p.m. and try to make sure we eat dinner by 7:30. I usually start preparing dinner the night before. If not, I get take-out on the way home. Don does not like to eat leftovers."

"So when do you get to rest?"

"After I put the dishes away and clean up. I stay up with Don, typically past midnight, before we retire."

"What about weekends?"

"Oh, there's usually laundry, grocery shopping, church, meetings, etc. I try to rest when I can."

"Are you happy with your life?"

"Well, I'm doing what I'm supposed to do. Isn't that what life's all about?"

"You mean life is about taking care of other people?"

"Yes."

"What about taking care of yourself?"

"Isn't that selfish? We are Christians."

"Really? Explain."

Gwendolyn grew up in a Christian home. Her father was clearly the head of the home and submission was a big issue. She never remembers her father ever speaking directly to her. He would always send messages through an intermediary—her mom or her brother—even when she was in the room. When he died, he left everything to her brother, instructing him to be fair to his sister.

"All my life, even as a young child, I always needed someone to tell me what to do. *Just tell me what to do and I will do it.* However, lately I have been losing my confidence in my ability to please everybody. Seems like the harder I work, the more demanding they get. I feel guilty all the time because I can't keep up. I feel like a big failure. I think everyone can see that. I am so afraid I could lose my job and let my family down!"

The savior or martyr complex is another key manifestation of the orphan syndrome in relationships.

Men tend to have the savior complex and are driven to take care of everyone, yet feel angry and frustrated with the heavy load no one has imposed on them.

Women like Gwendolyn exhibit the martyr complex, sacrificing their own needs to take care of others. Often the only escape is through illness—physical or emotional.

These two conditions are opposite sides of the same coin of doing for people, hoping to be loved in return. The problem is, even when love is offered, it is not enough to override the pain of being "on" all the time.

Deep sadness, loneliness, perfectionism, mood swings, lack of basic trust, chronic guilt, escapism behaviors, workaholism, inability to detach from outcomes, messiah complex, martyr complex, and a deep sense of unworthiness are all expressions of a crushed spirit. They are orphan traits.

Thankfully, there is hope and healing for those who are willing to take the journey.

# The Expression of a Healthy Spirit

A man's spirit sustains him in sickness, but a crushed spirit who can bear?

(Prov. 18:14 NIV)

What are the traits of a healthy spirit? Worship, trust, abandonment to divine providence, love and devotion to God, self and man, and resilience in the face of tragedy are some of the traits of a healthy spirit. The capacity and imperative to give and receive forgiveness is a potent characteristic of a healthy spirit also. It helps us release past hurts, entrust our future to God, and live purposefully in the present.

A common thread in the stories I share in this book is the choice to *trust* in the justice of God. Everyone has a different life story, some horrific, some not. However, we all carry within us the most potent power to heal—the power of forgiveness. However, this power is only activated when we surrender to God's empowering grace. This grace then allows our spirits to be purged and purified, our souls washed clean from the stain of bitterness and hatred, and our bodies released from stressful demands of self-preservation. We can then choose to live again—not as spiritual orphans—but as overcomers, sons and daughters of the Most High God, unafraid to connect again with our human family.

Let's take an in-depth look at what a healthy, functioning spirit looks like. Most believers are familiar with the functions of the physical body and the soul. However, few understand the spirit, and therefore, fail to identify it when it is malfunctioning.

## A Healthy Spirit Enables Us to Connect With God

Genesis 2:7 NIV, reads, "The LORD God formed the man from the dust of the ground and breathed into his nostrils the breath of life, and man became a living being." *Merriam-Webster's Dictionary* defines "spirit" as the life principle. It is the inherent part of us that is infused by God.

"We have not received the spirit of the world but the Spirit who is from God, that we may understand what God has freely given us" (1 Cor. 2:12 NIV). So the spirit is the "heart" or governing center for the whole man. The Bible enjoins us to, "guard your heart, for it is the wellspring of life" (Prov. 4:23 NIV). It is the seat of our character, will, personality, and mind. It is often referred to as the "inner man."

Since the spirit is from God, it cannot die. Therefore, we can say we are "spirits having a human experience." As the common expression goes, "We are spirits, we live in a body, and we have a soul." We know the body is appointed to live for a certain time on earth and then die (see Heb. 9:27).

Those who study the body, are often amazed at how magnificent it is. Scripture tells us we are "fearfully and wonderfully made" (Ps. 139:14 NIV).

The body has many redundancies and systems that work in perfect harmony, enabling us to physically navigate through life.

Recently, I had two surgeries on my left eye that took place within six weeks of each other. The eye surgeon cut, probed, stuck in tubes, and grafted tissue. Lying there observing the "abuse" being inflicted on my eye, I feel it's a miracle I have 20/20 vision today.

The regenerative powers of the body are amazing. Yet we know, when the body dies it starts to rot and is buried, returning to the dirt where it came from (Gen. 2:7). If the body that is destined to rot and return to dirt is so wonderfully made, it is unimaginable how splendid, awe-inspiring, and durable our spirits are! After all, our all-knowing Creator designed our spirits to last for eternity, like *him*. Just as the body functions to help us get through life on earth, the spirit also functions to help us get through this life, and also experience heaven even while on earth.

The fundamental function of the spirit is to enable *communion* or connection. It's a *relationship*!

The spirit empowers us to connect first to God, then each other. Finally, it helps us stay integrated, maintaining the connection between spirit, mind and body. Jesus refers to these distinct parts of us when he commands us in Matthew 22:37-40 (NIV) to:

> "Love the Lord your God with all your heart and with all your soul and with all your mind." This is the first and greatest commandment. And the second is like it: "Love your neighbor as yourself." All the Law and the Prophets hang on these two commandments.

As a counselor, I have the singular privilege to enter deeply into people's pain when I am allowed to walk with them for a season. I wish I could say every encounter has a great ending. Too often, as we saw in Julie's story, some clients are too invested in their pain to make the inner shift required for healing and growth. Some people leave and never return. Others keep coming back, but they insist that God, his Word, or other people must change to suit their preferred outcomes—a futile endeavor. Still others endow their misery with a stamp of approval, constantly rehearsing their pain, which then continues to grow.

Thankfully, I have been invited into what appeared to be the deep winter of a person's life and instead found healing warmth and encouragement that blessed my own soul. I smile even now when I think of Sister Mavis. Her body was racked with cancer in the prime of her life, yet she comforted her family and friends as she prepared for her imminent death, insisting we all call it her "homegoing." In the end, she slipped away with a smile on her face as we worshiped and wept tears of joy, tinged with sorrow around her now empty, earthly suit. Sister Mavis had a healthy relationship with God.

## A Healthy Spirit Enables a Relationship with God

The "Westminster Catechism" poses a fundamental question: "What is the chief end of man?" In other words, why are we here? It answers, "Man's chief end is to glorify God, and to enjoy Him forever."[4]

The spirit enables us to have the revelation of who God is—the almighty, all-knowing, loving God who is worthy of worship. John 4:24 (NKJV) says, "God is Spirit, and those who worship Him must worship in spirit and truth."

The Spirit also invests us with the ability to know who we are in God, which is necessary to sustain an abiding devotion to Him.

> For you did not receive the spirit of bondage again to fear, but you received the Spirit of adoption by whom we cry out, "Abba, Father."
>
> (Rom. 8:15-18 NKJV)

This was such a radical notion in Jesus' day. We can call God "Daddy!" Orthodox Jews cannot even say the word Yahweh! No other religion even comes close to making such a claim. We are *sons*, not slaves or even servants. *Sons!* This revelation is necessary to support our worship, devotion, prayer, etc. We do not worship, sing, dance, or work to get salvation. We sing, dance, worship, and work *because we are saved!* It gets better.

> The Spirit himself testifies with our spirit that we are God's children. Now if we are children, then we are heirs—heirs of God and co-heirs with Christ, if indeed we share in his sufferings in order that we may also share in his glory.
>
> (Rom. 8:16-18 NIV)

It is so much easier to *trust*—that is to say, have *faith* in a God to whom I can relate to as *Father*, than to relate to a God who is viewed as a punitive, cruel, aloof, and a judgmental taskmaster.

Clearly, our faith is also sustained by our ability to hear God (Rom. 10:17). Having the revelation of God as Father is necessary for effective prayer because we have confidence in our inheritance. We do not have to work for our prayers to be answered. We just have to *trust*—let go and let our Father do it for us.

## A Healthy Spirit Enables Connection with Others

The spirit imbues us with the ability to have communion with each other. When most people think of communion, they think of a ritual or ceremony in which bread is eaten and wine is drunk in remembrance of Christ. For many, it is a rote ritual, devoid of significance or power. In fact, many churches have communion services just a few times a year. However, communion has deep roots in Christianity. It goes back to the very first line in the Bible—"In the beginning God . . . (Gen. 1:1). The word for God mentioned there is *Elohim*—a singular God with three distinct expressions. "Let us make man in our image," says Genesis 1:26 NIV. We serve a God who lives in community—the Father, the Son, and the Holy Spirit—living together in deep mutual knowledge and intimacy, and always working in tandem—complete unity and agreement.

Our spirit is endowed with the same capacity and need for mutual connection and care or communion, which means, "intimate fellowship or rapport," according to *Merriam-Webster's Dictionary.*

Out of this "God place" in us, we can reach out a caring hand to other people. Thus, we are able to share in each other's joys, pain, suffering, and even be vulnerable with each other. We can be broken before each other. The word "care" is rooted in the Gothic *kara*, which means "lament." It connotes "crying out with, grieving and experiencing another person's sorrow" as Henri Nouwen expresses it in *Out of Solitude: Three Meditations on the Christian Life.*

Prior to the fall, Adam would speak of Eve as "bone of my bones and flesh of my flesh" (Gen. 2:23 NKJV). The two shared a deep intimacy as an outflow of acceptance without judgment, being naked and not ashamed. The ability to be kind, compassionate, and forgiving all requires a healthy spirit. We can endure our cross like Jesus did—not my will, but God's will be done. So our capacity to empathize and be present with each other is a spiritual function.

Former President Jimmy Carter evidences the beauty of a healthy spirit and how it is able to form deep connections with others.

"I am perfectly at ease with whatever comes," Jimmy Carter told reporters on August 20, 2015 at a press conference in Atlanta. Carter, ninety, went on to explain he had been diagnosed with stage-four cancer after a recent liver surgery. The cancer had spread to his brain and required immediate and aggressive treatment. Death could be imminent.

Watching the press conference, I was struck by the deep sense of confidence the former president exuded. His innate joy, especially in the face of such news, was palpable. He smiled and even cracked jokes throughout the event.

When he got the diagnosis, Carter recalled thinking he only had a few weeks to live. He did not succumb to despair and anger. He remained in good spirits and felt "surprisingly at ease." He went on to credit his resilience and grace under fire to his faith in God.

"It's in God's hands," he said with a smile. This was a man who was deeply at peace with God and with man, and grateful for a life well lived.

The following Sunday after the press conference, Jimmy Carter taught Sunday school at his church in Plains, Georgia, just as he had done for years. CNN reporter, Nick Valencia, highlighted the stories of some of the people who had camped out all night, driven hundreds of miles, or even flown in from overseas to be a part of the class. People came in from as far as Ghana and Guatemala. There was even a mother who had driven eight hours to show her son—also named Carter—"something special." Meeting the former president would be Carter's first birthday present.

During the class, Carter described *love* as the backbone of Christianity and exhorted the audience to trust God to help them through challenges and the inevitable painful seasons of their lives.[6]

At a time when gloom, despair, and quiet desperation seem so prevalent, Jimmy Carter reminds us of a more excellent way—living life purposefully and joyfully, even in the valley of the shadow of death. He personifies the innate transcendence of the human spirit when plugged into God's spirit.

Baptized in love, he is thus released from the yoke of bitterness, despair, anger and regret. Yes, Jimmy Carter has had his share of heartaches and deep disappointments. His parents and all his younger siblings fell to cancer. However, he remains unbroken and his spirit continues to sustain him. He chose the way of *love*, and God crowned his heart with his peace—a peace that "surpasses all understanding" (Phil. 4:7 NKJV).

President Carter's life is animated by a basic trust in God, a deep connection and abiding commitment to Rosalyn, his wife of sixty-nine years, and gratitude that fuelled his relentless work to help people around the world. Jimmy Carter lived in that place long before the world saw the remarkable display of grace under fire.

That same grace is available to all of us today.

## A Healthy Spirit Navigates Us through Time

Spirits are eternal so they can exist both inside and outside time as we know it. A healthy spirit can remember the past, live in the moment, and experience the future all at the same time. Thus, the capacity to navigate through time is a spiritual function. It enables us to move from "This is my story, this is my song," to "praising my Savior all the day long" (to quote Fanny Crosby), in my blessed assurance about the future.

Without this attribute, we are "stuck in affliction," with our souls refusing to be comforted (Ps. 77:2). We walk sightless among miracles and live in constant fear of the future—existential angst.

A healthy spirit allows us to participate in each other's lives for a reason, a season, or a lifetime, and be fully present through all of the seasons.

## A Healthy Spirit Responds to Conviction

Aleksandr Solzhenitsyn has written that the line between good and evil "cuts through the heart of every human being."[5]

I have been blessed to live in several cultures during the course of my life. In every one of them, it is wrong to kill the innocent or to steal from another. Through our spirits, God provides *light*, which becomes our moral compass. "The spirit of a man is the lamp of the LORD, searching all the inner depths of his heart (Prov. 20:27 NKJV). The degree to which we yield to that light determines our moral aptitude.

The Holy Spirit, using the agency of our spirits, serves as our "inner umpire," using God's supernatural peace to guide our decisions and actions.

A healthy spirit has the ability to receive correction and guidance without resisting and shutting down. This is absolutely necessary for growth. In fact, the ability to receive correction is a hallmark of sonship. "The Lord disciplines the one he loves and he chastens everyone he accepts as his son" (Heb. 12:6 NIV).

Neither fear nor love is an effective deterrent to sin—*conviction* is! It is that inner understanding that one has violated and overstepped spiritual boundaries, and has grieved him who is holy, and moved beyond the limitations set for humanity, whether fully understood or not. Conviction creates the ability and willingness to ask for and give forgiveness, change course, or repent when we sin.

## A Healthy Spirit Brings Connection and Wholeness Within One's Self

Our ability to overcome the inevitable storms of life is directly in proportion to the health of our spirits. We can be resilient in the face of fierce opposition—and still be standing when the dust settles. This requires oneness with the self. In other words, the mind and heart must be aligned. Too often, we dissociate from life circumstances, not allowing our hearts to connect with what our minds have to face every day. God wants us to be strengthened in our inner man in order to be able to trust him in our valley experiences. Often, the Lord is not looking to calm the storm on the outside. Rather, he wants to calm the storm on the inside so we can take his hand and trust him to walk us out of the storm.

Sometimes life throws us a curve ball at birth. Christian author Frank Peretti—dubbed the master of supernatural thrillers—was born with cystic hygromia. This rare defect produces fluid-filled sacs that form around the neck, as a result of a defective lymphatic system.

This condition required multiple surgeries and lengthy hospital stays, leaving scars on both body and soul. Between surgeries, Frank's tongue would swell and hang out of his mouth, oozing a disgusting, dark fluid. He drooled constantly, leaving dark stains on his chin, clothes and pillow. Eating, swallowing, and even speaking became progressively harder to do. He was hard to look at and consistently drew stares.

Frank's parents were devout Christians who did everything they could to help him. They even took him to an Oral Roberts healing crusade in Seattle, but the miraculous healing they prayed for did not come. The Perettis did not give in to hopelessness and despair. They continued to trust God and believe for their son's healing, even as they sought treatment for Frank's condition. They also encouraged him creatively.

By the time Frank was old enough for school, the disease had taken its toll. He was smaller than normal and talked funny, so school was hell. He was constantly taunted and called ugly names. Kids spat on him, kicked him from behind, and mocked his appearance. Physical education class was the worst. He was tripped, hit with towels on his private parts, and subjected to indescribable verbal and physical cruelty.

There was no exit ramp—quitting school was not an option. The constant insults with no respite eventually seeped into Frank's soul and wounded his spirit. Repeated, unrelenting assaults to his dignity eventually consumed the wellspring of faith, hope and love deposited into his heart by God, family, and friends.

But, God *always* enables us to overcome in his name. It was a process that took time, but Frank Peretti not only overcame, but allowed God to use his experience to bring healing to countless others trapped in the quagmire of bitterness and disconnection unleashed by abuse.

After the shootings at Columbine High School in 1999, Peretti, then in the fifth decade of his life, tapped into pain that had been transformed to power and gave poignant voice to the anguish of the nation and the world.

At a Life on the Edge Conference in Ontario, California on May 22, 1999, Frank Peretti found the courage to step out of his comfort zone and speak poignantly from his heart about the terrible toll that bullying and abuse had taken upon his life.

As he described it later, "This was a deep digger; a grave opener that scraped off layers of dirt, revealing issues that had been buried long ago, but were not really dead." That talk would eventually lead to a broadcast on *Focus on The Family* and the writing of his seminal book *The Wounded Spirit*.[7] This book has helped millions of people find the courage to acknowledge their wounds, step out of the grave of self preservation, give voice to the pain, connect with the community of wounded healers, forgive and receive forgiveness, and expand the circle of love.

## A Healthy Spirit Receives Inspiration

The word inspire literally means to *inhale*. We carry within us the potential to continue the creative process out of which we were birthed (Gen. 2:7). The same animating Source who breathed into dirt and formed man continues to breathe into us today, guiding us to create great works of art, music, sculpture, as well as knowledge to unlock the mysteries of the universe.

A prime example of this gift is captured in Michelangelo's words: "I saw the angel in the marble and carved until I set him free." Inspiration comes though the agency of the spirit to help us see, hear, discern, observe, feel, and translate what the mind of God is regarding a particular project or assignment. You know a work is inspired because it *moves* you, and creates an innate desire to worship the One who alone animates and brings life out of nothing!

All of these different functions of the spirit were robust and whole before the fall. Like the Godhead, there was no shade of difference between God's view and Adam's view. They co-created Adam's world. God created and Adam gave them names.

Since Adam carried the triune God's relational, connective essence, none of the beasts of the field, nor paradise itself, could satisfy Adam's need for suitable companionship. When Adam who was created by love, in love, for love, first laid eyes on Eve, in a moment of inspired awe, he exclaimed, "This is now bone of my bones and flesh of my flesh; she shall be called 'woman,' for she was taken out of man" (Gen. 2:23 NIV).

At that moment, the institution of marriage was birthed, offering us the possibility of enjoying the same deep communion the Father, Son, and Holy Spirit enjoy. Adam and his wife were both naked—completely transparent to each other—and felt no shame. Even so, we can be completely naked and open before God, and not be ashamed. By design, we were meant to have perfect communion with Him.

# FOUR

# From Order to Disorder

A s a counselor, I see clients who have the means to create their own versions of paradise, yet these dear souls live in abject misery because they are spiritual orphans, separated from the sustaining love of God.

It all started with "the fall." The fall refers to the first sin of Adam and Eve, which unleashed judgment upon mankind and nature. Since then, things have progressively moved from order to disorder. The most detrimental effect of all was that man was *separated* from God, becoming a spirit separated from his Creator, Father, and Sustainer. Man became orphaned in paradise, in a place that was the embodiment of pure joy and abundance!

The fall unleashed a tidal wave of other consequences. Chief among them is the incapacity to receive, transmit, and communicate love. It is impossible to worship, hear, or relate to a God from which one feels separated. As a believer, it is assumed we have unhindered communion with him, being translated from darkness to the kingdom of light. We are in a position where the Holy Spirit bears witness with our spirit that we are the sons of God.

However, here lies the main symptom of the orphan syndrome: the potential for intimacy and communion is created, but our spirit remains *unresponsive* because it is wounded. A person can be saved, and still experience this separation. Our spirit man is redeemed, but it does not connect and remains resistant to love. Although surrounded by the love of God, it pushes away that for which it truly longs. It is like the adopted child who refuses to be loved by his adoptive parents. An invisible wall remains between them from previous pain and hurt. Though they live in the same house and eat the same food, fellowship remains shallow.

How does one even pray, feeling no sense of connection to the Divine?

## My *Diem Horribilis*

One morning several years ago I woke up in abject horror. It was bar none the lowest point—the nadir—of my journey of faith. Alexandra, my wife of only a year had died unexpectedly a few months earlier. In the throes of my grief, I had allowed Satan (adversary, opposer, Father of Lies) to pierce my grieving, wounded spirit with his choice weapon—*lies*. Chief among those lies was that God is not worthy of my love and devotion. After all, why would a good God allow me to go through "hell," then satisfy my lonely, longing soul with a truly suitable helpmeet only to then yank me into the abyss a year later? Nursing those thoughts and resentments over months culminated in my *diem horribilis*.

That morning when I awoke, I could not sense God's presence for the first time since I was six years old. It was horrible. I had neither the desire, nor the ability, to pray or cry out to God. I tried to read the Scriptures, but quickly abandoned the effort, because the words were meaningless and lifeless to me. This intense fear was so all encompassing I could barely breathe. The angst was exacerbated when I started trying to analyze and control my breathing. I began gasping for air as I struggled to breathe. After a while, which seemed like an eternity, the word "fleece" flashed through my mind.

"God, if you are real, please have Bubba call me today." Bubba personified his name. He was a beefy, good ole hillbilly from Houston by way of Arkansas whom I had met some years back. He had been a total alcoholic who had been delivered and set free. After being set free, he began operating a chain of rehabilitation facilities, giving hope to other addicts. Bubba and I were close ministry partners for a season, but we had gradually drifted apart as our ministry interests diverged. We had not spoken in over two years at this point. I had tried to call him several times in the past, but all his numbers were disconnected or changed.

"Please God, let me hear from Bubba . . . please, if you are real!" That was the only prayer I could mutter.

The hours slowly, grindingly, passed.

Then my phone rang. It was Bubba. "Hey, Diddy!" That's what he called me.

I don't remember much of the conversation, but the joy of the Lord flooded my soul as I wailed in gratitude for God's mercy and love in my life. When I neither wanted to hear, nor reach him, entrapped by my own foolish stubbornness, the great God of the universe stooped down and descended into my situation. He rescued me from the well-laid out plans of Satan to destroy my life.

I made two determinations that day: first of all, God is good. Period. Second, I do not know what is good or bad.

Therefore, I refrain from judging myself, others, or God. Since then I have really been enjoying my walk with God!

## How Did I Get to That Dark Place?

Most suffering is the result of the judgments we make. The pain of my wife's death had created a deep ache and loneliness in my heart. The pain drove me to the end of my theology. I had gone to church, tithed, read the Bible, submitted to spiritual authority, and abstained from sexual immorality. I did not drink, smoke, or chew, but, without warning, disaster struck! I found myself walking in darkness (Isa. 50:10-11). Rather than trust in God (to whom the darkness is as light), I chose to light my own fires. I swallowed Satan's bait. I judged God and concluded he was unjust, and unfair.

## Reverse Conversion

In his book, *Halftime,*[8] Bob Buford, an entrepreneur and founder of Halftime Institute, recounts what he termed "The Hour of Reverse Conversion." He was born into a household of faith. He never doubted the existence of God and "always believed that Jesus is who he said he is." He credits the Lord with this unshakable faith. However, he goes on to describe a "reverse conversion" experience when he was fourteen years old.

His father had died when he was eleven, leaving behind a young widow and three young boys. Mom carried on with the media business in spite of the odds against women at the time. She drilled young Bob in the minutiae of the business, grooming him to take over when the time came. Buford recounts that his mother's dogged determination "produced both excitement and tension within me—a titanic, internal tug-of-war between leading a life of success in business, and leading a life of service in ministry." He vividly remembers making a decisive choice at age thirteen—preaching, baptizing, marrying, and burying were out, and making money as a TV executive was in.

"I had made a clearheaded (albeit) teenaged decision to put myself in the driver's seat of a turbocharged car." Buford would go on to drive that car into the president and chairman's seat in the family's media empire by age thirty-one!

God eventually redeemed the call on Buford's life. He has a high-impact ministry today. However, the wound of losing his father, coupled with his shift in judgment concerning God, kept him in a place of hindered communion with the Father for a season.

Many people are not aware of how much resentment they truly carry toward God and others. When we experience loss or trauma, the heart has to process these events somehow. They don't always get processed correctly.

Often, displaced anger towards God causes us to resist his love, leaving our spirits lonely and starving for love. Displaced anger is often displayed through judgments and vows. We may make statements like, "I'll never give my heart to anyone again," or "I can't trust anyone," or, "God helps everyone but me." In so doing, we put ourselves in a prison where we cannot access love on the outside and it cannot access us on the inside.

A woman I counseled who experienced a trauma in her childhood displays this very well. When Barbara and her husband arrived at my office, she was defiant and defensive as her husband explained the reason for their visit. They had been married for over thirty years, founded a thriving church, and raised three children who were now grown, married, and had their own families. He said the children had met with him recently and emphatically insisted that their mother seek counseling or lose all ties to her grandchildren. They were going to boycott all family functions until then. Their issue was that their mother was too controlling.

When it was Barbara's turn, she categorically denied the allegation. She listed in detail all the children's accomplishments, and the success of the church, as the fruit of her dogged diligence. She said, "I firmly believe you do not do anything unless you do it right!"

She said, "This whole drama has been orchestrated by our oldest daughter because I won't allow the grandchildren to bring their dogs into my home!" She just did not believe that people and animals should cohabitate that closely.

After she was done speaking, I asked her a question.

"Barbara, would you rather be loved or be right?"

"What kind of stupid question is that?" she shot back without answering.

I then invited this precious couple to pray with me, seeking God's counsel on the matter. As I prayed, I felt the nudging of the Holy Spirit. *Ask her about a childhood puppy.*

I hedged initially—unsure about the source of such a seemingly irrelevant insertion. But it was clear God was saying, *Ask her about the puppy.*

So I asked her, "Barbara, did you maybe . . . way back . . . have a puppy?"

"Puppy, what puppy? I told you I hate animals, especially dogs. Puppy? I can't stand puppies!"

Then her face began to contort and she began to wail—deep sobs punctuated by heartrending moans. She was clearly experiencing a deep emotional reaction right there in my tiny corner office at Prayer Mountain in Dallas.

Her poor husband looked at me with a "what-have-you-done?" look on his face. I shrugged and encouraged him to move close and comfort her.

I left the room, dejected, and feeling very insecure about my ability to hear God. I sat by the gazebo nearby and began to repent for presuming on God.

After about ten minutes, her husband came for me. His wife had stopped crying and seemed composed. Barbara went on to tell us a heart-wrenching story.

She was born and raised on the Colorado/New Mexico border. Her mother was a sweet and meek lady, while her dad was hardworking, but a raging alcoholic. When she turned five, in a moment of kindness, her dad bought her a puppy as a birthday present. In short order, the puppy became the life of the household. She slept with it, played with it, and shared her joys, pains, and dreams with that puppy.

Several weeks later, her dad came home drunk and angry. When she and the puppy did not get out of his way fast enough, he viciously kicked the puppy. As Barbara screamed, her father became even angrier. He went into his shed, grabbed a shovel, and proceeded to bash the puppy on the head, leaving a trail of blood, brains, and fur.

The five-year-old girl continued to cry in terror at the sight of her new puppy lying there, mangled and dead. When her screams were spent, she could only utter pathetic whimpers. Her father then dug a shallow grave and ordered her to shove the remains of her puppy into the hole.

Now crying softly in my office, Barbara continued to describe that fateful day. She recalled "seeing" herself leave her body, get into the hole, and wrap her little five-year-old arms around the broken puppy. She became "other" that day.

She closed her heart off to love. She made a subconscious vow never to allow anyone or anything to have the power to hurt her like that again. She chose to never be a victim.

That vow fueled a drive to be the "biggest dog" in every setting, in order to avoid pain. Yes, she'd built a successful ministry at the expense of her most precious relationships—first with God, her husband, and then her kids. Although she had led thousands of people to Christ, she always felt alone and lost. She was wounded and never received healing. She could not call God "Father" in a personal way. She tried hard to love and respect her husband, but believed he was weak. She fulfilled his needs more out of duty than affection or compassion. As for the children, she drilled into them, "There are no freebies in life—period!"

All the walls of self-protection and self-preservation began crumbling that day in my office. Barbara is now a doting grandmother, devoted wife, and above all, a loving daughter of the Most High God.

Recently my wife and I had the privilege of ministering to a group of men at the Eastham Maximum Security Prison near Lovelady, Texas, notorious because some of its occupants over the years included (Bonnie and) Clyde. Under the auspices of the Ministry Church, led by Dr. Paul and Jeri Carlin, I had been invited to teach a seminar on "Healing the Wounded Spirit" on Saturday, and then to preach on Sunday.

At dinner the night before the seminar, Jeri Carlin had asked my opinion about different issues the men in the new class of inmates presented. "Bro. Nick, what causes people to completely disconnect from other people? There's a man in the class you are teaching tomorrow who told me he does not feel connected to any other human being. In fact, he has not had any visitors in years, and he does not care."

"Well, Ms. Jeri, I believe that man has a wounded spirit."

That Saturday, about a hundred men clad in white filed in the newly renovated chapel and sat classroom-style in a comfortable room in the north wing of the prison. These men were currently enrolled in an accredited degree program in Bible studies. Among them was an associate pastor of a well-established mega church in Dallas, and an anointed worship pastor with a master's degree in music.

I taught about the spirit, its functions, the fall and its consequences—especially separation from God. I gave examples of vows people make to take the reins when their spirits are wounded or grieved. We then broke for a sumptuous lunch of baked potato stuffed with Texas brisket and a fat apple "dessert" washed down by sweet peach-flavored tea.

During lunch, Dr. Carlin approached me with tears in his eyes. He pointed at an inmate, a good-looking man with piercing blue eyes and a crew cut in his late fifties or early sixties. Dr. Carlin beckoned for him to join us and asked him to repeat the story he had just told him.

The man whom we had been discussing the night before now stood in front of me.

Sitting there in that classroom that Saturday morning, the Holy Spirit had transported him back to the moment when he "snapped" (his words) and quit caring.

He was six years old and it was Christmas. His step-dad had returned from the war or some other assignment. He was in another room, while the rest of the family—step-dad, mom, and two younger siblings—were in the living room. He heard his step-dad giving presents to his siblings. He heard their excitement as they opened up their presents. When his mom asked her husband about presents for him, his step-dad replied, "I've forgotten that he exists."

"I snapped that day, Bro. Nick. I just quit caring."

By age twenty-two he had shot and killed a young lady without remorse. He hurt many other people along the way. "I have been on death row and came close to being executed several times. The truth is, I welcomed it, 'cos I did not give a damn—until now."

Now he understood when and why he had snapped. It had all come full-circle for him. That day he made an intentional decision to open his heart again to love.

"Snapped, horror, reverse conversion, die" are terms and expressions of the same experience—heartbreak or a wounded spirit.

Trauma speaks and it usually demands an urgent response. Since the fall, our default position in times of pain is separation from the One we believe is supposed to keep us from pain. Of course, Satan takes advantage of this pain, inducing dialogue to accuse God of not caring for us. When we buy his lies, we then turn toward self and lose our sense of communion with God and with others. We become obsessed with protecting and providing for ourselves.

## Why the Enemy Loves Trauma

In his seminal book, *Heartbreak and Heart Disease,*[9] cardiologist and counselor, Dr. Stephen Sinatra, describes heartbreak as "the emotional response to the loss of love and intimacy in life . . . It creates a bent towards self, lays the foundation for a character structure/personality with acute fear of rejection and resistance to love." What a profound statement!

In a moment's time, trauma and heartbreak have the power to shift our paradigms, beliefs, and spiritual relationship. Lucifer works actively throughout the lifecycle to create as many lonely orphans as possible in his unrelenting war against God and mankind. There is nothing he can do to separate us from God and his love, but he works at keeping us unresponsive.

This orphan syndrome is a mindset, a mentality, a worldview or perspective. The essence of it is:

*You are on your own.* This mindset is rooted in lies. Thoughts come to mind such as:

- Don't expect any freebies.
- Life is about competition—for power, money, position, respect, fame, etc.
- Every day presents a choice to be predator or prey.
- You can't really trust anyone, you *have to depend on yourself!*

Life is also about protection and provision.

At a basic level, we are all born into this. For some, it was aggravated even before we were born. For many, it is inflamed by circumstances surrounding our birth. For others it is compounded by how we were raised.

But, for all of us, every hurt or heartbreak throughout the lifecycle creates a wounded spirit, taking us from order to disorder, and increasing alienation with God and others, until that wounded spirit is healed.

# Heartbreak Through the Lifecycle

Surely I was sinful at birth, sinful from the time my mother conceived me.

(Ps. 51:5 NIV)

Heartbreak and trauma do not only happen during and after childhood. They can happen much earlier—even in the womb. The impact of trauma can go far beyond what we can remember, leaving us with symptoms and manifestations later in life.

This is evidenced even in basic scientific studies. In an experiment in a laboratory in Boston, a pregnant mouse was kept on a near-starvation diet. As expected, her babies were unusually small at birth. Those baby mice later developed diabetes, even though they were raised normally.[10]

Another example proves the same hypothesis. The Dutch famine ("hongerwinter") happened in the German-occupied, densely-populated western region of Holland during the winter of 1944-1945. The Germans cut off food and fuel supplies to millions of people. Thousands died as a result. This tragedy created the environment for a natural experiment called "The Dutch Famine Birth Control Study." Dutch scientists discovered the children of pregnant women exposed to famine were more vulnerable to diabetes, obesity, cardiovascular disease, micro albuminuria, and other health problems. As expected, these children were small at birth, and their own children were also smaller at birth. This suggests the famine the mothers experienced caused some kind of change that was passed on to the next generation.

One of the affected children, actress Audrey Hepburn, spent her childhood in the Netherlands during the famine. She later suffered from anemia, respiratory illness, and edema as a result. She also suffered from clinical depression (which is also associated with malnutrition) late in life.

I just love it when science confirms God's wisdom and just upends long-held theories and hypotheses. Remember John the Baptist leaping in his mother's womb, Jacob and Esau fighting in Rebecca's womb, and the prophecies! Biological determinism and "tabula rasa" theories have been mantras in science for a long time. Epigenetics—meaning above, or on top of genetics—suggests otherwise. Our genes can be activated and deactivated by signals from the environment. This environment includes our conscious thoughts, emotions, and unconscious beliefs (for example, repressed vows). So our thoughts, attitudes, and perceptions are major determinants of what genes are turned "on" or "off."

Your beliefs impact your biology! This applies throughout the lifecycle, from birth until death. Now let's examine how certain traumas can wound our spirits, impact our beliefs, and thereby negatively impact our lives, especially our ability to connect to God and to each other throughout the lifecycle— until healed. Remember, it's not always what happens to you that matters. It's as much how you react to the hurt or trauma. What did you walk away with? How did your beliefs change?

## Prenatal Wounds

I recently attended a memorial service for a young man whose mother had attended one of my workshops on "Overcoming Rejection" some years earlier. During the seminar, I specifically talked about how "botched" abortions could impact survivors throughout the lifecycle.

During the break, his mother shared with me she had tried to abort her son. Her husband was away at war. She had a six-month-old daughter and then discovered she was pregnant. Young, scared, and overwhelmed, she sought counsel from some older ladies. She was counseled to sit in a bathtub infused with mustard, as well as to try other invasive procedures to induce an abortion.

Nothing worked. Her son was born anyway.

As a baby he seemed to resist love and affection. He would resist hugs. He lived like a stranger in the family—always on the outside looking in. It was as if there was a solid glass wall between him and others, especially his family members. He drifted away from home and got caught up in drugs and the rock scene.

After my seminar, his mother apologized to him and ministered healing in some specific ways I had suggested. Things improved some, but he never seemed to get over the hump.

At the memorial service she said he was still seeking reassurance that he would make it to heaven. He was still unsure, although he had already put his faith in the finished work of Jesus Christ on the cross. This poor soul, thankfully now with Jesus, could not get past a wound inflicted upon his spirit resulting from an attempted abortion.

Some would wonder how he could process the botched abortion, since he had not even been born. The spirit of a man is what animates the body. The spirit is alive and communes with the outside world even before the mind is fully developed. Therefore, at any stage in life—including pre-birth—the spirit can be wounded.

Other sources of prenatal heartbreak include, but are not limited to:

## Rape

Can you even begin to imagine how conflicted a young woman would be after finding out she's carrying the child of her rapist—the man who brutalized her body and shattered her soul? Even in cases of non-stranger rape, the consequences are severe for mother and child. I have counseled with mothers who were raped by their husbands/boyfriends during a difficult time in their relationship. After the children were born, they usually have a really hard time connecting with other people. They are typically angry and alienated from family and society.

## Maternal Depression/Mental Illness

By definition, depressed people have limited engagement with their world—including their baby in-utero. In addition, serotonin and other hormonal deficits are baked into the fetal development. It may be the template for the development of a pervasive pessimism throughout the lifecycle.

- *Gender disappointment:* What happens when a husband really wants a son (presumably, an heir), and his wife is desperate to grant his wish. Then, when she conceives, they are ecstatic until they find out they are having a girl. He is disappointed, but supportive, while she is devastated and feels as if she has failed him, and is grieving over the "wrong" baby in her womb.

- In my work as a counselor, I have been amazed at the number of people who still struggle with rejection, feeling invalidated by both parents because they were the "wrong" gender. Typically, it is fathers rejecting daughters, but I have seen the reverse. These wounds can affect gender differentiation/preferences later in life.

- *Conception after miscarriage:* Imagine a baby who makes it full-term after mom has a series of miscarriages. By the third pregnancy, she is, at best, tentative about the viability of her current baby. How much of her heart does she withhold in case she loses this baby, too? How is the baby experiencing this reticence? Most likely as compassion deficits and primary rejection.

## Post-Natal Injury

### Adoption

Imagine being whisked away right after birth by strangers and taken to another room. You are given a warm bath and then placed on the bosom of another stranger who then proceeds to nurse you with a bottle. Welcome home, you have just been adopted at birth. All the familiar sounds, smells, moods, movements, textures that decorated your world for nine months are gone forever, now replaced by strange objects, smells, sounds, and rhythms.

How does the baby cope with that?

The adopted child is now presented with a nasty bouquet of issues such as rejection and abandonment by birth parents, and a deep sense of the unworthiness of love. The adopted child also carries a sense of guilt for grieving the absence of birth parents, while also carrying a sense of disloyalty to adoptive parents.

Sometimes there are many significant physical, cultural, or even ethnic differences between the adoptee and the parents. These differences become more pronounced as the child grows older—leading to an even deeper sense of disconnection and inner loneliness.

Children adopted later in life also experience these feelings. Often they are ill-equipped to make the necessary journey of self-discovery in their teenage years. Usually, they do not have access to their roots. This reality has psychiatric implications as they grow older.

Adoptees are often caught between a desire to find their biological parents and remaining loyal and grateful to their adoptive parents. Life is difficult enough for people born into loving, nurturing families. Imagine starting out with such a deck stacked against you.

Adoption is an orphan-syndrome factory. However, it can be healed. I know many adoptees who are leading productive and wholesome lives today.

## Injuries During Childhood

### Sexual Abuse

Children are not little adults. They are powerless, have smaller organs, less blood volume, less developed brains, and fewer coping mechanisms. Therefore, children are very vulnerable to the weaknesses or wickedness of their parents or guardians. They are also more susceptible to changes in their environments.

Few childhood injuries go deeper than the injuries associated with sexual abuse. This occurs far too often.

I once took some time off and went to Naples, Florida to write. While I was there, I got one of those phone calls that counselors dread. One of my clients called to say she was on her way to the doctor's office with her young son. While bathing him that morning, he cringed when she tried to wash his bottom. Upon further inspection, she felt compelled to take him to the doctor. I held my breath. I supported her as best as I could, being fully aware that hers was one side of the story. (There is usually another side and the truth somewhere in between the two).

However, even after twenty-five years, I am still shocked by the human propensity for perversion and evil often disguised under the banner of love. Sexual abuse is even more shocking when perpetrated by parents, family members, or close family friends.

The NBC program *Dateline* "To Catch a Predator" impersonated underage children who then lured "would-be" pedophiles with the promise of sex. The pedophiles were then confronted. The program was filmed in locations across the country and confronted a wide swath of society—registered sex offenders, firefighters, teachers, rabbis, ministers, coaches, Homeland Security officers . . . the list goes on across all demographics!

The statistics are all over the place, but the general consensus is about one out of five girls and one out of twenty boys is a victim of childhood sexual abuse.[11] The exact prevalence is difficult to pin down because incidents go unreported for a myriad of reasons.

In my years as a counselor, I have found nothing else leaves more stretch marks upon the soul than childhood sexual abuse, besides active-duty combat soldiers or veterans scarred by the blight of warfare. Childhood sexual abuse violates the body, shatters self-governance, darkens the soul, and ultimately breaks and alienates the spirit. It is indeed pernicious.

A little girl went to bed every night, dreading the footsteps that inexorably make their way toward her bedside.

Every night she prayed and asked God for it to stop. It did not. The abuse went on for two years! The little girl finally stopped praying. Instead, she began staring at her own broken body from a perch on the ceiling. She has since become "other." Her step-dad—a pastor—was supposedly tucking her in at night with Bible stories.

Childhood sexual abuse is like a cluster bomb. A single act, or a series of violations, each contains shrapnel loaded with lies about God, our identity, as well as lies about divine care and providence. It is truly a weapon from hell. It is a very efficient orphan-maker.

Unless healed, childhood sexual abuse effects typically persist throughout the lifecycle. They include, but are not limited to:

- Difficulty with intimacy; an inability to connect due to lack of trust
- Poor body image; sees body as damaged or grotesque
- Overwhelming feelings of guilt, shame, and deep sadness
- Loneliness, depression, anxiety
- Protective weight gain/loss (obesity or anorexia)
- Promiscuity or aversion to sex
- Gender/sex confusion
- Codependent relationships
- Violent sexual fantasies
- Self-destructive and even suicidal behavior
- Sometimes hostility toward God and religion
- Very low self-esteem
- Fear of losing control; the need to control others creates further alienation
- Dissociative disorders
- Higher vulnerability to rape and other sexual violence later in life

When I work with victims of childhood sexual abuse, the question I am asked most often is, "Why did God allow this to happen?" or, "Where was God when I needed Him?"

We will discuss healing and God later. However, it is important that all pain is vented. Someone needs to weep with them and for them. This begins the healing process.

Besides childhood sexual abuse, there are many other threats to the health of our children. These include emotional, physical, verbal, and spiritual abuse, and even divorce. It is imperative that we amplify issues involved with their wounded spirits.

It is interesting that when we are children, we spend a lot of time, energy, and resources trying to avoid, suppress, and even repress anything that causes us discomfort or pain. As we get older, we then spend untold amounts of resources (therapy, self-help books, groups, spirituality, friendships, etc.) trying to restore, resurrect, inflame, and nurture the very attributes we worked so hard to destroy in childhood.

To lead emotionally intelligent and fulfilled lives, empathy, sympathy, compassion, gentleness, meekness, love, joy, peace, patience, goodness, trust, and faith must all be cultivated again.

The essence of successful parenting is to help children balance pain and pleasure as they grow up. They must be taught how and when to suffer legitimately, for their good, as well as the common good. They must learn to develop the capacity to suffer now and enjoy later. Finally, they also must learn self-regulation and delayed gratification.

Heartbreak is not limited to childhood. It can happen throughout the span of life, including in the womb. Many of us have experienced relatively happy childhoods, and were healthy individuals—until injury happened in adulthood.

# Divorce: The Great Divider

Man who is born of woman is of few days and full of trouble.

(Job 14:1 NIV)

Love is to human beings like oil is to cars. Without oil, car engines lock up and quit. Humans, on the other hand, have found ingenious ways of living without love. Of course, our insides groan, our minds race constantly, our hearts ache, yet we find countless ways to distract ourselves with counterfeit loves.

There are many sources of pain in adulthood. Divorce is a major one that involves both the broken covenant and the consequential separation of a married couple. Divorce takes other forms, even if a person is not married. For the purpose of this section, we will view divorce as the separation or severance from people, as well as places and things we once loved.

As I researched the latest statistics on divorce, the story of Scott Young popped up. According to London's *Evening*

*Standard*, Young, previously known as one of the UK's wealthiest men, fell sixty feet to his death. The body of the fifty-two-year-old tycoon was found impaled on the iron railings outside the $4.7 million rented London home he shared with his girlfriend.

Scott Young was in the middle of a very bitter divorce from his ex-wife, Michelle, making the rounds of the British courts for seven years. Michelle believed that Scott was worth a few billion, while he insisted that he was bankrupt and penniless. In August 2013, Young was sentenced to six months in prison when he refused to disclose the details of his fortune. He was also ordered to pay his ex $31 million dollars, but his ex says she hasn't received a penny from the settlement.

Michelle said Scott had attempted suicide and subsequently entered into treatment after they separated in 2006. Young left behind two young-adult daughters. "We have been to hell and back," she said.

Some of the words the newspaper used to describe this incident are: "impaled, distraught, loss, grieve, death, bitter, battle, ex, dragged, courts, split, settle, victim, meltdown, prison, suicide, treatment, leaves behind, daughters, *hell*."

God hates divorce (see Mal. 2:16). It destroys the concept of covenant that is so paramount in our relationships with God and with each other. It also nullifies the ideal template for producing and nurturing godly offspring. Jesus said, "Moses, because of the hardness of your hearts, permitted you to divorce your wives, but from the beginning it was not so" (Matt. 19:8 NKJV).

Sadly, I can describe this injury from both sides of the spectrum—as a child, and also as an adult. I was a young teenager when my mother left the family. As she had promised to return, the separation was even more devastating as the months and years slipped by without this happening. I again experienced the devastation of divorce when my wife of fifteen years left for a trip to visit her mother in New Jersey, planning never to return, having met another lover online.

Psychologist Judith Wallerstein tracked a group of children of divorce from the 70s into the 90s. She interviewed them at different stages of their lives, from five to twenty-five years after the divorce. She discovered the effects of divorce linger on well into adulthood and are especially poignant when these children start dating seriously. The effects of divorce include:

- The shattering of a child's sense of safety in the world. Mom and dad, those two "superhumans," modeled failure that typically involved fighting, harsh words, betrayal, and sometimes violence.
- A child's sense of rootedness is ripped apart and he/she has to adapt to all kinds of different people and relatives as each parent attempts to rebuild his or her life.
- These kids harbor a deep sense of abandonment.
- A deep feeling of divided loyalties on the inside.
- Anxiety about commitment in romantic relationships, which may persist throughout life.

Divorce is the great divider—it rips apart the seed-bearer from the seed-giver. The one who used to be the keeper of the secrets of your soul is now your enemy. God hates divorce. Satan—the opposer of God and the accuser of man—is only too eager to use this "war of the roses" to divorce people from God, each other, and their children.

The hearts of the fathers often turn away from the children. This dynamic creates orphans until these wounds are healed by *love*.

Of course, there are some marriages so toxic the children are poisoned by the mutual contempt, and damaged for life. Still, the issue there is not the institution of marriage, but rather the hardness of men's hearts that creates and sustains these situations. Typically, such couples are divorced in their hearts, but continue to live together for religious or economic reasons.

I believe most—maybe all—marriages can be saved if both partners are willing to save it. Too often, people want their situation to change, but they do not want to change themselves.

One can cast all the other issues we face as adults into the context of divorce, that is to say, a total or radical severance of people or things that were once closely connected. Most of our pain is the result of such loss in one form or another:

- Loss of a job that we loved and cherished for many years. It defined our day as well as our friendships and sometimes our identity. It is especially brutal for men who have spent over a decade on a job, then lose it.
- Separation from our life savings/investments by unscrupulous money managers, bankers
- Loss of loved ones through death or strife/conflict
- Loss of faith due to offense taken with God or Christian leaders
- Loss of health and vitality after a devastating diagnosis
- Loss of a sense of safety through rape, war, burglary, or other dastardly acts of violence perpetrated by another.

Again, Satan, the opposer of God and the enemy of man, uses these situations to isolate, harden, and dislodge souls from vital connections to the human family. We make conscious or unconscious vows such as:

"I do not need love."
"I will never allow anyone to hurt me again."
"I will never trust again"
"I will not feel pain."

Like Adam and Eve, who ate of the Tree of Knowledge of Good and Evil, once we eat of the "tree of judgment"— judging God to be bad because of our circumstances, judging others as damnable and refusing to offer forgiveness, or judging ourselves as unworthy of love or affection—we become disconnected. We become *orphaned*.

Most of us react to these losses by gradually closing our hearts to love. C.S. Lewis aptly captures this sad dynamic: "The only place outside Heaven where you can be perfectly safe from all the dangers and perturbations of love is Hell."[12] Consciously or subconsciously we make vows that imprison our spirits and cause us to fall into a state of perpetual grieving for paradise lost.

Do you know why we almost never talk about heart cancer? That's because cardiac tissue does not divide once it is cast in utero. God designed it to be *unitary*—no divisions, singular in focus!

A haunting soulful ballad by Rose Royce called "Love Don't Live Here Anymore" about abandonment and vacancy becomes our anthem. We then attempt to fill that vacancy with our own counterfeits that never satisfy. Jeremiah 2:13-14 (NIV) says:

> My people have committed two sins: they have forsaken
> me, the spring of living water, and have dug their own
> cisterns, broken cisterns that cannot hold water. Is Israel
> a servant, a slave by birth?

When we flee from God (love) we imprison our spirits in the very cages that we built to protect ourselves from pain. We became spiritual orphans with no expectation of an inheritance. We then have to strive and bust our gut for everything. We see competition everywhere. We become independent and self-reliant. Our hearts are closed to love and connection. We end up with controlling and superficial relationships, and a deep inner loneliness we try hard to conquer. It never goes away, until we surrender to God's love. Our lives become marked by traits of restiveness and overextension, performance orientation, the hero-complex, angst, nexus, and oppression.

# Moving from Doing to Being

Where is the life we have lost in living? Where is the wisdom we have lost in knowledge? Where is the knowledge we have lost in information?

(T. S. Eliot, *The Rock*)

## Restive and Overextended

"Super Joe" has piercing green eyes and roguish good looks that mask the steely tenacity in his heart. He was a throwaway baby, adopted by a man he describes as insulting, untrusting, and undermining—a man who would embrace you and stab you at the same time—a man who couched sadistic tendencies under the umbrella of religion. His adopted mom, bless her heart, was basically raised as an orphan. She had long checked out about having any personal opinions. He had two siblings who were truly their father's children—entitled and disengaged. Raised in the East Texas ethos of "no gimmes in life," he channeled every hurt into work and sports. As soon as it was legal, he "got out of Dodge," determined to make a name for himself, and "get rich or die trying."

From very meager beginnings, and with a strong determination to succeed, he worked in the mines of Canada, the jungles of Guyana and Belize, and eventually the sandpits of East Texas to become a millionaire with assets north of $139 million—all before he turned forty-five years old. He has the trappings that go with such success, of course. He has the beautiful wife, well-appointed mansion, stocked pond, hundreds of acres of land, horses, boats, planes, a private airstrip close by, and a fleet of expensive cars.

However, what does "Super Joe" do on a typical day? He spends his time in his big, often muddy, truck trudging through different plants and troubleshooting. He is up at the crack of dawn, has his devotions, eats breakfast in a hurry, kisses his wife and kids goodbye, and is gone chasing after the next big deal. He is gone all day; his phone rings nonstop. Some of those calls are to encourage friends or employees in dire straits and even win some souls to Christ. But it is constant motion.

He finally makes it home at dusk and maybe eats dinner with the family. But wait. He has to confer with business partners in South Africa about a deal in Zimbabwe. Then, there are calls to make to Australia, Israel, Singapore, or elsewhere in different time zones. Finally, Joe grabs some sleep and repeats the cycle the next day.

The simple definition of the word restive is "unable to stay still." This is usually because of impatience, dissatisfaction, or boredom. It connotes a sense of restless uneasiness. It's like having "ants in one's pants"—being fidgety.

Restive is an interesting word because its meaning has undergone a reversal. It originally meant "inclined to remain still." However, the word eventually became associated with horses refusing to move. Imagine riding a horse, and the horse sees an obstacle or a dangerous animal. It balks and refuses to continue the run. The horse does not just stop and sit there, no, it fidgets; it's nervous and jumpy.

So it is with orphans. Somewhere on the journey of life, some traumatic event caused a broken heart, which in turn caused the person to become uneasy all the time. The normal rhythm of life (i.e., pulsation and then relaxation or systole/diastole, night/day) is disrupted. These individuals are on all the time, even at night. This may actually be profitable for a while, as they channel this "energy" into creative endeavors; however, with time, it leads to burnout and other serious consequences. After all, we are human *beings*, not human *doings*. Orphans typically do not know how to rest—how to *be*.

In the creation sequence in Genesis, there was evening then there was morning. Then on the seventh day, God *rested*. The Jewish theologian, Abraham Heschel explained it best in his book, *I Asked for Wonder*:[13]

> In the tempestuous ocean of time and toil there are islands of stillness where man may enter a harbor and reclaim his dignity. The island is the seventh day, the Sabbath, a day of detachment from things, instruments and practical affairs as well as of attachment to the spirit.

In nature, there is a time of hibernation, when things slow down for a season. For orphans, there is no rest for the weary; there is no off-ramp until healing comes.

Psalm 107:23-30 paints a vivid picture of the turbulence that can hit any life at any time. Using the metaphor of a merchant ship caught in a storm, the psalmist goes on to describe the frightening terror the sailors felt. At their wits end, they cried unto the Lord and he brought them out of their distress. They were grateful for their rescue, but that's where the relationship ends. Since orphans do not trust anyone, even the Lord, they would not allow him to guide them to their desired haven, their safe place. They cannot say what David said in Psalm 16:5-6 (NIV):

> Lord, you alone are my portion and my cup. You make my lot secure. The boundary lines have fallen for me in pleasant places; surely I have a delightful inheritance.

Sons and daughters understand inheritance, orphans do not. They feel compelled to trust their gut for everything; therefore, there is no time to rest the mind. Neither fame nor fortune can assuage that restiveness.

Elvis Presley was born in 1935 in Tupelo, Mississippi. His twin brother, Jessie Garon Presley, was stillborn, so Elvis was raised as an only child. His talent, good looks, silky voice, and infectious sensuality catapulted him into über-fame at a fairly young age. As he approached middle age, and began facing the nostalgia of Paradise lost, he turned to sycophantic doctors and mood-altering drugs to medicate his restiveness. He needed drugs to keep him awake and drugs to put him to sleep. These included uppers, downers, and powerful painkillers such as Dilaudid, Quaalude, Percodan, Demerol, and cocaine hydrochloride in quantities more appropriate for those terminally ill with cancer, according to Joel Williams in *Salon* (Nov. 16, 2014).

Toward the end, the man could not stand one minute of life with a sober mind. All the medications could not quench his restiveness. "The King" died on August 16, 1977.

Fast forward to June 25, 2009 when another "king" died of acute propofol and benzodiazepine intoxication after suffering cardiac arrest at his home.

"Do not try to remake Thriller" is now a metaphor for attempting to recreate perfection of a bygone era. The pressure to come back bigger and better, coupled with his tortured relationship with his father (orphan spirit) created the seedbed for the kind of restiveness that does not allow for rest.

Michael Jackson paid a doctor $150,000 per month to "put him down" every night and wake him up the next morning.

I could add the stories of Whitney Houston, Marilyn Monroe, and John Belushi to the sad list of tragic "superstars."

This inability to rest comfortably in one's skin is not just limited to celebrities. There is no geographical solution to a spiritual problem. It hurts to believe we are unloved or unlovable. It hurts to feel alone and disconnected from God and others. It hurts to believe people love us for what we do for them, and not just for who we really are. It hurts when love becomes inexorably tied to perversion and pain. It hurts when we lose vital connections before we even have the words to express our pain. In the end, our bodies weep the tears our eyes refuse to shed. No amount of money or fame can assuage that kind of inner restlessness. Only the revelation of divine connectedness and the crazy, uninhibited love of God can heal us.

One of the things that "Super Joe" enjoys doing at home is plucking the ticks off his favorite dog, "Killer" (the rest of the family calls him "Miller") and watching the ticks burn at the end of a lit matchstick. He feels a strong kinship with Killer, a rescue from the shelter that is not particularly good looking, but brave and very loyal. Killer has taken a few snakebites intended for his owners. The snake usually won the first battle but Killer always won the war. His head would swell up to the size of a basketball. He would lie down for a few days, but so far he has bounced back after about a week. He has that fighting spirit; that dogged determination to win the war, no matter the cost.

One of "Super Joe's" prized possessions is a picture of a J-Dam bomb with his company's name written on it (in ink) that was dropped on one of Saddam Hussein's palaces. He fondly remembers a time when he seriously considered putting together a mercenary army to overthrow the leaders of a banana republic who had double-crossed him on a lucrative mining deal. That's "Super Joe"—heart of gold, man of steel and *restive*!

## Consequence of Restiveness: Overextension

It is very easy to confuse service for God with service to God. Service to God is marked by *waiting*, standing before God, and abiding in Him until He gives instructions to move. Service for God is marked by fleshly striving to achieve whatever elevates us in the eyes of the world under the guise of ministry. It is the hallmark of the orphan spirit. Orphans cannot be still. The torment of risking being exposed as insecure and decrepit drives people to scheme, plot, strive, strategize, and claw their way to the top of the "Tower of Babel."

The sons of Zadok in the Old Testament were faithful priests. It is worth noting they had a father, Zadok, who took time to "father" them into the Lord's service. They understood the power of trusting, letting go, and detaching from outcomes, because they knew that God, our Papa, Abba, Daddy, had them covered. They understood the concept of inheritance. They offered the Lord the fat and the blood. The blood was for the propitiation of sin; the fat was to satisfy the Lord. The blood obliterated the old; the fat ushered in the new. The sons of Zadok dwelled in the secret place of the Most High, secure in their inheritance—no striving, no scheming. Their ministry came out of the "no sweat zone" from a position of rest.

The unfaithful priests—orphans—were in the outer court dragging the sacrifice to the altar, slaying it, and offering it to the Lord. They were constantly preoccupied with the next promotion, extra provision, rules, regulations, reputations, etc. They plotted and even twisted the instructions to advance "the kingdom." Their conversation was typically about ministry connections and the size of the "bribe offering" needed to gain personal access to an even greater orphan. Waiting quietly before the Lord was labeled as laziness and cast as a lack of ambition.

We find this preoccupation with busyness and restiveness still in the church today. Only in the church do we fail to understand that serving God is not the same as knowing God. In any organization, there may be laborers who work for the boss, but that does not mean they have a relationship with the boss other than what they do for his business. Orphans do not understand this concept. So we are left with many church leaders, elders, and ministers who do a lot, but are unable to commune with the one they are working for.

I know of a high-octane preacher once considered a prince among his peers. Anointed—no doubt! He has an amazing capacity to pull impactful revelation out of the most obscure passages of Scripture, to the glee and approbation of awestruck congregants in churches around the United

States and the world. His congregants reward his gifts well. His lavish lifestyle is commensurate with his fame. Then his mother died. He was definitely a mama's boy. He was told to slow down, and take time to grieve, but *no*! Instead, he scheduled forty preaching engagements in forty days. He followed in the footsteps of another celebrity preacher who once quipped, "Who needs to sleep—sleep is stupid!"

To this, I emphatically say, "No sir! Burnout is stupid!" Orphans burn out and eventually flame out. Sons operate from a position of rest and typically end well.

Another believer I met wakes up at dawn each morning. She faithfully has her devotions. She drops off her grand-daughter at daycare and goes to her office in the center of a violence-prone part of town. There she advocates, counsels, exhorts, mediates, and educates until dusk. She then picks up her granddaughter—usually a couple of hours late, fixes dinner, drops off her granddaughter at the evening sitter, and then attends a church or civic function at least five days a week. Between engagements, she is constantly on the phone putting out fires or catching up on another project. Relationships? Who has time! She is *holy*!

Even nations can be ensnared in this "busyness" ethos. In the 2014 Cadillac ELR commercial, actor Neil McDonough portrays a wealthy guy showing off his toys as he lambastes those who take longer vacations. He walks around his pool, then through his fancy home as he lectures the audience about why America works so hard.

"For stuff? No, because we are crazy, driven, hard-working believers."

He then talks about what sets America apart—Americans going to the moon who then stopped going because they were bored but left the keys in the lunar rover because, "We're going back."

McDonough says, "You work hard, create your own luck, and got to believe anything is possible." Then he chides other countries for taking four weeks of vacation a year, while Americans take two, saying with a wink, "That's why we are a great country, *n'est-ce pas?*"

Wherever you go, whatever you are doing, you still take your spiritual problem with you. Orphans live for the moment. They maximize moments and string them together, squeezing every ounce of fleeting satisfaction as they try to outrun their ever-present inner loneliness.

Sons see their inheritance set aside even before embarking on an enterprise. No high water, fierce opposition, or unpopularity can quench the assurance of a predetermined outcome already set aside for them. Sons are content to wait for the full manifestation of their inheritance.

They are willing to make personal sacrifices, if necessary. They are not interested in creating a moment. They want to start a *movement*, a work that leaves an inheritance of faith, love, peace, and provision for the next generation.

## How to Achieve the Same thing Without Sacrificing Everything

In *Running on Empty*,[14] Fil Anderson tells a story of an investment banker from a large city who was vacationing in a North Carolina coastal town.

Standing on a small pier one afternoon he watched as a lone fisherman docked his small boat. He had several yellowtail tuna inside the boat. The banker complemented the fisherman on the quality of his fish and asked how long it took to catch them. The local replied, "Only a little while." The banker then asked, "Why didn't you stay out even longer and catch even more fish?" The local said, "With this, I have more than enough to feed my family and share some with my friends." The banker then asked, "But what do you do with the rest of your time?" The fisherman said, "I sleep late, fish a little, play with my children, take naps with my wife, stroll into town each evening where I sip wine, and play the guitar with my friends. I have a full and busy life."

The banker scoffed. "I could help you. You should spend more time fishing, and with the proceeds buy a bigger boat. You could buy several boats. Eventually you would have a fleet of fishing boats. Instead of selling your catch to a middleman, you would sell directly to the processor, eventually open your own cannery. You would control the product, processing, and distribution. You would, however, have to move to a larger city, perhaps eventually to New York, where you would run your ever-expanding enterprise."

The fishermen, intrigued, asked, "But how long will all this take?"

Fifteen to twenty years," the banker replied.

"But what then?" asked the fisherman.

The banker laughed. "Here's the best part. When the time is right, you would announce an IPO and sell your company stock to the public and become very rich. You would make millions!"

"Millions?" The fishermen asked. "Then what?"

The banker said, "Then you would retire, moved to a small fishing town, where you would sleep late, fish a little, play with your children, take naps with your wife, stroll into town each evening, sip wine, and play the guitar with your friends!"

# Performance Versus Acceptance

Love that is conditional is not love.

Perfectionism is an effective way to slowly commit suicide.

(Nick Eno)

"Dad, you make me feel like a bad person. I am not a bad person. I have worked my butt off to be a good person, but that's not enough!" Those words hit me like a wrecking ball to my gut. I collapsed to my knees at the foot of the bed as my daughter continued sobbing.

*What? That can't be true!* My mind was trying to counter what my heart already knew was true. This is the one person I have loved and consistently carried in my heart since I first heard her heartbeat twenty-two years ago. Her words, however, had weighed my love and found it sadly deficient. The best of my love made her feel like a bad person.

I opened my mouth to speak, but began wailing—except no sound emerged. I was gagging for air and trying to reach out for her.

She was not done with me yet. "Dad, you are so busy helping other people. But you are human, too. Your mom left you, my mom left us. You just keep working!"

I finally crawled toward her and tearfully asked her to forgive me. I would later release her from my expectations, and plead with her to spread her wings and fly. I told her she had the right to be her own person. She should make her own choices and fail or succeed on her own terms. I owe her love— unvarnished, untethered *love*. Period.

One of today's most relevant Christian leaders, Tullian Tchividjian, Billy Graham's grandson, made these very poignant and astute observations:

> While the cross may be the symbol we treasure in Christianity, the way most of us Christians live is as if the symbol of our faith is a ladder rather than the cross. We've come to believe that the Christian life is a progression from weakness to strength—"started from the bottom, now we are here" seems to be the victory chant of modern Christianity.[15]

I bear witness to this in my own journey of faith, as well as in my ministry as a counselor. My recent encounter with my daughter shocked me to the core. It sparked a renewed desire to be really intentional about yielding to God daily so He alone can expand my capacity to love people his way.

It is very humbling to realize, after nearly three decades of "walking with God," I'm still not much of an improvement from my own father.

It was a life of privilege—mansion, servants, Catholic boarding school, and great trips with my dad. However, I remember only one intimate moment between us when I lay dying of tetanus.

My parents converted their bedroom into a hospital room and took care of me around the clock for several months. I saw tears in my father's eyes several times as he, a pharmacist, administered my drugs. My violent spasms made speech impossible then, but by his actions, my father showed me he loved me.

Yet I do not remember a hug or any intimate moments between us. I remember long letters full of instructions and admonitions. "I love you" was not part of his vocabulary.

I have been present in my daughter's life. There have been lots of hugs, saying of "I love you," and many celebratory moments over her amazing accomplishments over the years. However, when I am honest with myself, there was always an undercurrent of "you owe me"—loyalty, success, good behavior, honor, purity.

My heart breaks as I write these words. It pains me even more because performance-based "love" seems to be the rule and not the exception in the body of Christ.

## Pressing Expectations

Derek Prince, internationally acclaimed Bible teacher and spiritual father, who taught love to millions of believers around the globe, was dogged by the same "pressing expectation" almost all his life. In *Derek Prince: A Biography*,[16] author Stephen Mansfield does a brilliant job of capturing the essential elements that shaped his early life.

Derek Prince was born in India in 1915. He spent his first five years there before his mother took him to England and left him under the care of her parents while she rejoined her husband in India.

In 1915, India was part of the vast British Empire. Derek's grandfather, Robert, his uncle, Edward, and his father, Paul Prince, all served as officers in the extensive military apparatus needed to maintain control over 300 million Indians. Duty to country was paramount to these men.

Derek's father, Paul Prince, a captain assigned to the Royal Engineers, was away building bridges and advancing the king's realm for most of Derek's formative years. As was the custom, Derek was raised primarily by his Indian nanny, not his mother. What little time he spent with his parents was strictly scheduled and enforced. Thus, young Derek spent the first five years of his life as the de facto adopted son of an Indian woman.

However, as the scion of a prominent British family, he could not escape the weighty expectations. Duty to country, high moral standards, and loyalty to the rules of the realm, trumped family ties.

"A fatherly rebuke might begin with the words, 'As Kipling said . . .' only to be followed by several lines of the poem in answer to some transgression on Derek's part," writes Mansfield. Rudyard Kipling's poem "If" epitomizes the stiff upper lip and stoicism admired among the British of that era, and yet today. (In 1995, "If" was voted Britain's favorite poem in a BBC opinion poll.)

"Even in old age, Derek could lean back with his eyes closed and recite the poem 'If' flawlessly, tears streaming down his cheeks."

## IF
### Rudyard Kipling[17]

If you can keep your head when all about you
Are losing theirs and blaming it on you;
If you can trust yourself when all men doubt you,
But make allowance for their doubting too;

If you can wait and not be tired by waiting,
Or being lied about, don't deal in lies,
Or being hated, don't give way to hating,
And yet don't look too good, nor talk too wise;

If you can dream—and not make dreams your master;
If you can think—and not make thoughts your aim;
If you can meet with Triumph and Disaster
And treat those two impostors just the same:
If you can bear to hear the truth you've spoken
Twisted by knaves to make a trap for fools,
Or watch the things you gave your life to, broken,
And stoop and build 'em up with worn-out tools;

If you can make one heap of all your winnings
And risk it on one turn of pitch-and-toss,
And lose, and start again at your beginnings
And never breathe a word about your loss:
If you can force your heart and nerve and sinew
To serve your turn long after they are gone,
And so hold on when there is nothing in you
Except the Will which says to them: "Hold on!"

If you can talk with crowds and keep your virtue,
Or walk with Kings—nor lose the common touch,
If neither foes nor loving friends can hurt you,
If all men count with you, but none too much:

> If you can fill the unforgiving minute
> With sixty seconds' worth of distance run,
> Yours is the Earth and everything that's in it,
> And—which is more—you'll be a Man, my son!

This is the ultimate orphan's anthem! Who can fulfill all those ifs?

Contrast that with Matthew 5:5 (NIV): "Blessed are the meek, for they will inherit the earth." There seems to be a belief indoctrinated in our sin nature that love is always conditional. We lean towards performance instead of acceptance; towards conditions instead of surrender. As Mansfield rightly pointed out, it is a very stirring poem, but it is all about the external life (life in the outer court). It's about actions, dexterity, strength of character, etc. There's nothing about the inner life, the spirit of a man—who that person really is.

Derek Prince would struggle with the tension between the inner and the outer life for most of his days. Healing would come much later.

Jacob in the Old Testament had a dream at Bethel (Gen. 28:10-15). In this dream, Jacob saw a stairway leading up to heaven with angels ascending and descending on it. Above it, stood the Lord. The Lord proceeded to speak a blessing over Jacob—a blessing that included provision, protection, and a sure inheritance to last for all time. It was an unconditional blessing, a covenant the Lord vowed to bring to pass of his own accord. Jacob, a deceitful liar, was chosen, not because he deserved it, but simply because God sovereignly chose him.

Jacob woke up from his sleep, acknowledged that God had visited him, and even built an altar to commemorate the visitation. Then came the big "if" in verse twenty.

> Then Jacob made a vow, saying, "If God will be with me, and keep me in this way that I am going, and give me bread to eat and clothing to put on, so that I come back to my father's house in peace, then the LORD shall be my God."
> (Gen. 28:20 NKJV)

*If* God will do these things for me . . . What part of "I have given you," didn't Jacob get? Jacob then proceeded to offer the Lord a "bribe," a hook.

The supplanter, schemer, or orphan cannot receive. Maybe it is because he cannot give without strings attached. Jacob himself was raised in a home where the parents had favorites among the children. Isaac loved Esau because, as a hunter, he performed in the field. Jacob on the other hand was his mother's favorite. Coming from a culture dominated by preference and rejection, it was easy for Jacob to assume "there are no freebies here!" God can't possibly bless me just for being me. He knew who he was and who he had become.

The orphan always wants reassurance in the form of deals, bargains, or contracts, to create a structure of safety. Relational faith is hard to come by.

It would take Jacob twenty years and multiple heartbreaks to get another opportunity with God for healing. After Jacob came to the end of his own striving for significance, he finally found rest in God and his name was changed to Israel. He did not prevail in the struggle, he prevailed in holding on, resting, trusting, and abiding after his hip socket was dislocated (Gen. 32:22-32).

Recently, I watched a movie called *The Judge*,[18] starring Robert Duvall and Robert Downey Jr., essentially the story of a tortured father/son relationship, with Robert Duvall playing the judge.

After a rather difficult childhood, Hank, played by Robert Downey Jr., the middle son of three boys, leaves his little town in Indiana and eventually becomes a very successful attorney in Chicago. In spite of his outer success—Ferrari, model wife, sweet young daughter—his life is in turmoil. When his wife is unfaithful he becomes very conflicted. When Hank gets a call to go home because his mother has died, a set of events is set up that would change both father and son.

While home, Hank gets dragged into defending his father in a trial for a hit-and-run accident where the judge is accused of a murder. The harder his son tries to defend him, the harder he tries to sabotage his own case. The raw animosity between father and son is palpable throughout the movie. The judge just flatly refuses to affirm his son as a man, or even as a great attorney.

The judge goes to prison, is eventually released on medical clemency grounds, while Hank settles down in the little town. The movie ends with father and son fishing together from a boat in the middle of the lake. Just before he collapses and dies, the judge finally looks at his son and tells him he loves him and that he is the best attorney he ever knew.

This poignant story is one of a family struggling to find the vocabulary of love and to express it to each other. Think of all the energy wasted and the years steeped in animosity and inner loneliness. The only vocabulary the story characters knew was that of performance. "What can you do and how well can you do it?"

Dr. Stephen Sinatra said, "If acceptance is based on achievement, there is an avoidance of intimacy, contact and commitment."[19]

"Super Joe" called one evening, asking for prayer for his dad who had just suffered a heart attack. Of course, he made sure his dad was offered the very best care at a regional hospital. The initial prognosis was not good, but things got worse the next day. Two relatively younger patients on either side of his dad's room were taken out of the hospital feet first.

In our conversations during this trying time, I encouraged this son of a "dyed-in-the-wool" Southern Baptist preacher to anoint his dad with oil and pray the prayer of faith for his healing.

One night Joe did just that.

"Bro. Nick, I did not know what I was doing. I applied some oil on my hand and slapped it on his head. I prayed like I have never prayed before. It was like an out-of-body experience."

His dad left that hospital alive and is still alive as of this writing.

"Super Joe" also told me he had confronted his father in that hospital room about never receiving a father's blessing. His dad broke down and told him he loved him and was proud of him. That longing in Joe's soul to be accepted without conditions was finally laid to rest. Joe is still basking in that blessing today.

We don't perform for God in exchange for his love. He is indeed willing to bless you, just for being *you*. That love can be received through relational faith. Relational faith means it is well between you and God. Relational faith says, my Abba Father loves me, just because I am me. Such love is there *before* the performance is accomplished, no matter what you do for him. God wants to give you the love of a father—unvarnished, untethered *love*. Period.

> The LORD thy God in the midst of thee is mighty; he will save, he will rejoice over thee with joy; he will rest in his love, he will joy over thee with singing.
>
> (Zeph. 3:17 KJV)

Just . . . rest.

# The Hero Complex

D
o orphans rule the world? Author Daniel Coyle explores this question in *The Talent Code: Greatness Isn't Born*[20]. This was also the question a French study posed. Coyle examines the work on eminent orphans of a clinical psychologist named Marvin Eisenstaedt[21].

In the 1970s, Dr. Eisenstaedt tracked the parental histories of people accomplished enough to merit at least a half-page entry in *The Encyclopedia Britannica*. He was testing a theory he had developed that posited genius and psychosis had a correlation to the loss of a parent or parents at an early age.

Eisenstaedt discovered the "parental loss club" was overrepresented among this eminent group. Political leaders who lost a parent early included Julius Caesar (father, at fifteen), Napoleon (father, at fifteen), George Washington (father, at eleven), Jefferson (father, at fourteen), Lincoln (mother, at nine), Lenin (father, at fifteen), Hitler (father, at thirteen), Gandhi (father, at fifteen), Stalin (father, at eleven), as well as fifteen British prime ministers. I add to that list Bill Clinton (father, infant), Barack Obama (never knew his father).

Many scientists and artists, from Copernicus and Newton to Michelangelo and Mark Twain, also make the list. These people are obviously not genetically linked so another factor must be responsible for this clear trend.

It turns out the smoking gun is losing a parent or parents. This is a strong signal that communicates to the child, "Hey, you are not safe!" This lack of safety then serves as a primal cue that unleashes a great amount of energy focused on safety and survival.

Eisenstaedt called this cue, "a springboard of immense compensatory energy." It is powerful enough to change the child's relationship to the world, redefine his identity, and focus his mind on the dangers and possibilities that life presents. The child learns to be self-sufficient early.

I venture at this point to propose a hypothesis that orphans rule the church also (small "c" church, not the Church universal). Anecdotally, I know the early histories of some pastors who are deemed to be "very successful;" they all lost a parent early.

Orphans seek to overachieve to make themselves feel safe, as well as accepted, and loved in this world. They usually have an edge in creating an aura of self-protection, but they lack in the part of life that requires love.

## The Hero of Albuquerque

Johnny Lee Anthony Tapia was born in 1967 and raised in a neighborhood described as a scary, deadly place. Told his father was murdered before he was born, he was raised by his mom until age eight. One Friday afternoon, his mother dropped him off at his grandparents' home. She said she was going to the dance hall. He remembers begging her not to go. They found her three days later, barely alive. She had been raped and stabbed twenty-two times with an ice pick and died four days later.

He remembers waiting at the door for his mom to come and pick him up. According to the HBO film, *Tapia,21* Johnny said, "Let's just say I'm still waiting at the front door for her. And she's never going to come back."

The murder was never solved, and his grandparents, who were very poor, raised him. Johnny described his grandpa as a "really rugged, tough, macho man." He was the head of the family of eight brothers and nine sisters. Johnny called them his siblings but they were his uncles and aunties.

His uncles used to make him fight in street fights for a dollar. He said he didn't like fighting, but it was normal to him. Around eleven years of age he tried boxing. In his first fight, he got a knockout in thirty seconds. "Since then I've never stopped," said Johnny.

He would go on to win five Golden Gloves and be rated number one in the world for six years in a row before he turned pro.

"My grandpa was a fighter. He was always there for me. I wanted to take after his footsteps. I wanted to be somebody."

Johnny Tapia turned pro in 1988. By age twenty-three he was the USBA Superfly weight champion. Undefeated, he was on the verge of breaking out as one of boxing's new stars.

Outside the ring, he still lived in a dark, dangerous world. He joined a local gang and began using cocaine. Later in his life, he'd refer to cocaine as his "mistress." His cocaine use stalled his career for several years.

During this time he met his wife, Theresa, and she became his rock, his anchor. Shortly after they got married, she locked them both in a small rented house, hoping he would dry out. He described the first three weeks as hell. He shook terribly as his body got rid of the cocaine. "I broke everything in the house. She said, 'Go on, go on, break it. You are going to fight very soon and you are going to pay for it all!'"

In 1994 he resumed his boxing career. He fought for his first world title shot on October 22, 1994 in his hometown of Albuquerque, New Mexico and won!

Johnny Lee Anthony Tapia was the hero of Albuquerque. He was now *somebody*. "Fans were crying for me. Everyone weeping. I was excited, happy. We hugged each other and cried . . . I did not do it by myself. I did it with my wife . . . Sorry I put her through hell . . . but she knew there was a better Johnny in me."

Tapia grew even greater in stature in Albuquerque when he vanquished a local upstart challenger—Danny Romero. They fought in Las Vegas in 1997 and Tapia won. "Johnny Tapia for President" banners, as well as loud mariachi music became standard fare before his fights. He was "adored" by the people of Albuquerque. He would go on to win five world titles in different weight classes.

But his life outside the ring was marked by several overdoses on cocaine, comas, and the death of his brother-in-law/trainer and nephew who were on their way to visit him in the hospital. He also spent time in prison.

Johnny also discovered his father was Jerry Padilla, a neighbor who was still alive. He fought his last fight on June 4, 2011 in Albuquerque with his father attending.

"I think if my mom was alive, I'd probably never have fought . . . She's taken care of me this far. Boxing has saved my life . . . I've been as low and been as high as you can get. I've always had a saying—'Yesterday is gone, if tomorrow never comes, today I'm OK.'"

On May 27, one month after his last interview for the HBO documentary, *Tapia*, Johnny Lee Anthony Tapia, "The Hero of Albuquerque," was found dead at his home at the age of forty-five. The official cause of death was listed as heart failure.

Johnny Tapia was the hero with a broken heart, a man driven by his pain most of his life. Despite his "hero" status, the heartbreak from the loss of his mother finally consumed him.

When pain or loss is not properly grieved, the body will create its own defense mechanism against the pain of lost love. According to Dr. Stephen T. Sinatra, author of *Heartbreak and Heart Disease*, "Heartbreak can literally hurt the physical heart." This physical defense mechanism is characterized by a combination of immobilization and rigidity of the chest wall, shallow breathing and muscular tension, creating cardiac stress that can eventually lead to cardiac arrest.

Dale Hansen, a great sports anchor in the Dallas area, put "hero" into perspective recently on his regular "Unplugged" broadcast:

> My heroes are the men and women who run into a burning house—the house we are trying to run from. The men and women who chase bad guys down an alley we would not go into. The men and women who answer the domestic violence calls, knowing they might very well get caught in the crossfire of an angry husband, only to be told by the woman there, "It's all a misunderstanding."

The same call keeps coming, the woman keeps saying the same thing, until she eventually can't say anything at all.

I don't defend police blindly. I'm simply defending the definition of "hero." I don't buy the argument that some police officers make . . . that they are just normal people like the rest of us. No, they are not. They have the power of God strapped to their right hip, and the power to use—sometimes questionably so—but they are special people who have made the choice to do a job most of us won't do. And that's a hero to me. Like the men and women who fight the wars I do not understand and do not agree with. But those men and women who choose to answer a country's call—a call most of us won't answer—those are the true heroes.

They're not paid millions for the job they do, and they don't complain when they're not paid millions more. They live amongst us. They teach in our schools. They work in our hospitals. There are heroes everywhere we choose to look, but I've never met a hero who played a game on Sunday, or played any game for that matter.[22]

Among the "ten thousand reasons" (from the song "Bless the Lord" by Matt Redmond) for my heart to sing praises to Jesus is the profound simplicity of his definition of hero—*the one who loves the most.*

Very rarely will anyone die for a righteous man, though for a good man, someone might possibly dare to die. But God demonstrates his own love for us in this: while we were still sinners, Christ died for us. Since we have now been justified by his blood, how much more shall we be saved from God's wrath through Him! For if while we were God's enemies, we were reconciled to him, how much more having been reconciled, shall we be saved through his life!

(Rom. 5:7-10 NIV)

Owe no one anything, except to love one another.

(Rom. 13:8 NKJV)

My command is this: Love each other as I have loved you. Greater love has no one than this: to lay down one's life for one's friends."

(John 15:13 NIV)

John and Paula Sandford, authors of *The Elijah Task* poignantly pointed out:

We often translate greater love has no man than that he should lay down his selfishness for his brother, or his ambition, or his own wishes. None of these things are life. They are death. We do not have life to lay down until we receive Christ's life. That is the life we are called to lay down.[23]

Orphans will try at times to put aside what is consuming them—their ambitions, their drive for success—to appease those closest in their lives. These sacrifices yield no fruit because they are born out of fear, out of our sin nature.

My buddy Joe does not have to be "super" for me to love him. He does not have to be a multimillionaire or the commander of a mercenary force to deserve love. If he had ended up alone in an orphanage and became a drug addict, he would still deserve my *love*—all of it. Johnny Tapia did not need to be "somebody" for me to love him. My wife and children do not have to perform heroic acts for me to love them.

We all deserve love because we bear the image of God, the *imago dei!*

Paul Tournier summarizes it well in *Escape from Loneliness*:

> Love is not just some abstract idea or feeling. There are some people with such a lofty conception of love that they never succeed in expressing it in the simple kindnesses of ordinary life. They dream of heroic devotion and self-sacrifice. But waiting for the opportunity that never comes, they make themselves very unlikeable to those near them and never sense their neighbor's need for affection. To love is to will the good for another. Love may mean writing with enough care so that our correspondent can read without spending time deciphering, that is, it may mean taking the time to save his time. To love is to pay one's bills; it is to keep things in order so that the wife's work will be made easier. It means arriving somewhere on time; it means giving your full attention to the one who is talking to you. To miss what he says means that we are more interested in what we are telling ourselves inwardly than in what he is telling us. To love is to try to speak in his language, even if we have mastered it but poorly, rather than to force him to speak ours.[24]

# Angst: Healing the Dread

If there is no enemy within, the enemy without can do us no harm.

(African Proverb)

Angst is a word that evokes pain even if you do not know what it means. It's a feeling of deep anxiety or dread, typically an unfocused one about the human condition or the state of the world in general. Synonyms of angst are: anxiety, fear, apprehension, worry, foreboding, trepidation, malaise, disquiet, disquietude, unease, and uneasiness.

This type of reaction makes sense in the context of a child who feels alone and without sponsorship in the world. Angst gets baked into the very fabric of the orphan's existence. Once in, it permeates everything and typically does not have the decency to dissipate even after the perpetrators pass on.

If we are unyielding to the persistent call of love, then we endow this usurper of joy, energy, and creativity with seeming immortality.

Orphans tend to possess the anxiety of children, but the anger and frustration of adults. It makes for some very contradictory situations: powerful teachers and preachers dogged by persistent oppression, world-class performers throwing up each time they are about to appear on stage, or mavens of toughness who cannot endure an airplane ride.

In Steven Mansfield's authorized biography of Derek Prince, Prince poignantly recalls a pivotal moment in his life. After living in India with his parents for the first five years of his life, his mother dropped him off with his grandparents in England, and rejoined her husband in India. Shortly after she left, young Derek was playing one day when he heard footsteps. Quite naturally, he thought, *Mother! She is home!* Not really. It was the maid. "The tears came as well as the crushing realization that he was all alone. His parents were a world away."[25] Prince goes on to say that a "pathological form of grief" invaded his soul at that moment—paralyzing, gnawing loneliness. It was an oppressive malaise that would persist until the last couple of years of his life.

Until recently, Super Joe's reaction to any perceived threat or rejection was to go into adrenal overdrive—a full-blown anxiety attack. He describes feeling so panicky he was certain he was going to jump out of his skin. Important meetings, long-planned vacations, and important milestones have been sacrificed because he was too anxious to make the flights.

He has spent countless sleepless nights in the grip of this unrelenting, gnawing, yet amorphous sense of foreboding. As he allows himself to bask in the glow of God's love and grace, Super Joe has gotten relief. He is also acquiring tools to help him override the acute symptoms. However, this "bad dog" still shadows him.

Most, if not all of us, carry deep wounds in our souls. They are too deep and we remain too attached to the source of the hurt to heal ourselves. Too often we are not even aware of these breaches. We are too busy trying to mitigate the symptoms.

> The purposes of a man's heart are deep waters, but a man of understanding draws them out. Many a man claims to have unfailing love, but a faithful man who can find?
> (Prov. 20:5-6 NIV)

Such wounds are typically healed through the ministry of a brother or sister in the Lord. As they gain our trust, we can then gradually bare our souls and find the grace and the courage to give and receive forgiveness. Hopefully, over time, we will learn to accept ourselves, free of harsh judgment.

In my seminars, I use the analogy of a minister as a vessel containing sanitizer. That is usually the filthiest container in the room by the end of the day. All squeeze the container to cleanse themselves, leaving their germy imprints on it. However, the vessel cannot sanitize itself. Someone else has to upend the container, get a good dose of its contents, and slap it all over the vessel to purify it. As we know, that's not always easy. Orphans do not allow many people to get that close.

> But we have this treasure in jars of clay to show that this all-surpassing power is from God and not from us.
>
> (2 Cor. 4:7 NIV)

Many believers live every day in the reality Jack Frost writes about in *Spiritual Slavery to Spiritual Sonship*. Frost draws from a February 1998 newsletter from Derek Prince:

> Every morning I would wake up with a sense of foreboding of something evil awaiting me. It was never anything precise. Just some amorphous darkness. This unknown evil never happened, but every day the foreboding was there . . . After I was baptized in the Holy Spirit, the foreboding diminished in intensity, but it never disappeared. I did; however, discover that if I set my mind to praise and worship, the foreboding will lift from me, yet it always came back the next morning.[26]

Pastor Jerry's wife drove him to my office. This beloved man of God was really in a bad place. He had not slept for almost two weeks. He was afraid if he closed his eyes, he might never wake up. He believed he was doomed to hell. It was very obvious to me he was in the throes of a "nervous breakdown."

As we talked, I learned the family had gone through a series of major transitions in the previous few years. They had finally settled into a familiar, albeit new, position. It became obvious Jerry was a student of God's Word. However, he was "perseverating"—always looping back to the same narrative of self-condemnation and hell.

I shifted to a more structured exercise, inviting his wife to participate in the session. Together we constructed a genogram or a map/lifeline of the most significant events in his life. Jerry was the oldest of three children. His father was a very gifted preacher/teacher who was also an alcoholic. He was loving and kind when he was "on" but very mean and demeaning when he was "off." He had an itinerant ministry and so was gone a lot. One day when Jerry was seven, his dad just went away and never returned.

The family moved to a small town in West Texas after his father left. Times were tough, but they used what they had and made what they needed. Over time, Jerry felt called to the ministry, attended a very conservative Bible college and was ordained by a holiness denomination. He really enjoyed pastoring and was evidently good at it. After a short time, he was the go-to guy to rescue struggling churches. He married and started a family.

After a series of unfortunate events, the leadership in his denomination was not pleased, and Jerry felt he had no choice but to resign from his post. When he turned in his resignation letter, his superintendent told him, "If you leave our denomination, you'll lose your inheritance, and ultimately your salvation."

He moved on anyway and prospered. In time, he moved to a large city in the Southwest and started a work that grew into a mega-church. He launched a fifty-million-dollar fundraising campaign to build a new church campus. The work consumed him. He was involved in every aspect of the enterprise, from financing, to design, to construction, and even interior decoration. He knew his family was suffering, but he had promised them a month-long vacation after the project was done.

On the eve of the grand consecration, he got a frantic call from his wife, the kind that every parent dreads. His seventeen-year-old Dawn, sweet baby Dawn, his angel from above, his only daughter, had overdosed on her mom's antidepressant pills and alcohol. As she was being rushed to the hospital, Dawn died in the ambulance.

That day in my office, several years later, the couple was still actively grieving and the tears flowed freely.

"I felt like a hole opened up right under me. I fell in and I have not been able to climb out of it ever since. All the pain I have been running away from since I was seven came crashing upon me all at once. In the past, I could always find the next project to occupy my mind. This time, I could not. I did not want to. Dawn deserved better. I blame myself. I could not function for several months.

"One day, the words of the old superintendent came back to haunt me, 'You are going to lose your inheritance and ultimately your salvation.'"

Jerry accepted a "buyout" from the church he founded. He moved to another city close to the mountains and started a couple of businesses. But he was not fulfilled. After a few years he accepted an invitation from an old friend to help stabilize a church that was floundering. He took it and did a good job and things seemed to be mending.

One day, he was driving home after a meeting, listening to a sermon on the radio. When he heard the preacher pronounce the same consequences for disobeying spiritual authority—no inheritance and loss of salvation—Jerry became completely unraveled. That led him to my office.

Remember, *there is no geographical solution to a spiritual problem.* Wherever we go, there we are. Nothing can be healed until we acknowledge we have a problem and confront it, hopefully with the support of counselors, mentors, friends, spouses, and of course, the healing power of God. As long as our buckets are full, Satan has the right to traffic in our unhealed wounds. He is delighted to torment us with fear, foreboding, and self-loathing.

Derek Prince goes on to say, in the previously mentioned newsletter:

> My experience of God was revolutionized by personal experience in 1996. Ruth and I had been sitting up in bed one morning praying together as we normally do, and I became aware of a powerful force at work in my feet and lower legs, and it moved upward until my whole body was forcibly shaken by it. Ruth told me later that the skin on my face changed to a deep red, but at the same time I was aware of an arm stretched out towards my head, seeking to press down something like a black skull cap upon me.
>
> For a few moments, there was a conflict between these two forces, then the power at work in my body prevailed, and the arm with the skull cap was forcibly taken away and vanished. Immediately, without any mental process of reasoning, I knew that I could now call God my Father. I had used the phrase "Our Father," for more than 50 years . . .

I believe Derek Prince was "baptized in God's love" that day.

Friends, we do not have to wait fifty years to get a personal revelation of God's "Abba" love for us. The evidence is all around us. We have to push past defenses and be willing to lay bare the torment in our hearts to a trusted, hopefully anointed, and competent minister.

Pastor Jerry had a few rough weeks as we processed the contents of his bucket. He took some time off to rest and reflect, and followed "doctor's orders," albeit reluctantly sometimes. (We Charismatics like to tough it out with God, but we need each other to find lasting wholeness. You never know through whose eyes God chooses to look at you on any given day!)

When Jesus prepared his followers for his imminent departure he told them, "I will not leave you as orphans; I will come to you" (John 14:18 NIV). He sent the Holy Spirit to indwell us and reveal the Father's love to us. He showed us we *can* walk victoriously as sons and daughters, and intentionally and consistently purge ourselves of those things that give the enemy any claim over our lives.

# ELEVEN

# Nexus: It's All About Me

My father always wanted to be the corpse at every funeral, the bride at every wedding, and the baby at every christening.

(Alice Roosevelt Longworth)

Orphans love the notion of being "well-connected." They never pass up an opportunity to name-drop or show off their connections. However, they do not seek connection in order to nurture or be nurtured. They seek connection to ultimately control or take over. It offers another layer of safety in an unsafe world.

There is another word that evokes a strong feeling even as you sound it out—*insinuate*.

On the surface it means: *to suggest or hint in an indirect or unpleasant way.* However, if you drill just a little deeper, it offers another meaning: *to maneuver oneself into a position of favor or office by subtle manipulation.*

We must remember the governing impulse of the orphan is a driving need to feel safe. Nothing assures security like being in charge and having the last say on every issue.

This explains why orphans are overrepresented in the pantheons of power in the world and I believe also in the church (remember, small c).

## Understanding Charlie

This is vividly illustrated in the personality of the fictitious Charlie—a highly motivated individual with a truly dysfunctional orphan spirit. Charlie seems to be charming and engaging with everyone. He has never met a stranger. On airplanes, coffee shops, or even at stoplights, he loves to make people feel as if they are the center of his world—at first. In a family, church, or business setting, he is always the first one to volunteer for a task. Once he gets the opportunity to participate in a project or assignment, he moves quickly to gather as much information as possible about the project, the people, their likes, dislikes, preferences, and hurts. He seemingly works very diligently and cooperatively with everyone.

However, as the project proceeds, he begins to selectively control what information goes where. He works hard to insinuate himself into every aspect of the operation, ingratiating himself with those in power. He loves to give expensive or special gifts to those in authority. He makes sure all notice his generosity of spirit. As he acquires more influence within the organization, he begins to subtly criticize, subvert, and undermine anyone who stands in the way. His ambition has no bounds. He truly believes he is the best at whatever he does, and that only time and impostors stand in his way.

When confronted, even over minor "facts," he will create his own "facts" and convincingly counter in a dramatic way. He will lie without the slightest hint of conscience. He is extremely good at turning the tables on anyone who would dare question his motives. He will play the victim at the same time he is destroying anyone who dares hold him accountable. He seldom, if ever, empathizes with other people. No matter how tactfully you approach him about any issue, it is never his fault. You must have misunderstood him, or you took it the wrong way. He seems incapable of feeling someone else's pain. He truly perceives himself as blameless—always. So you will never hear him apologizing for any specific offense. It is always proceeded by, "If I hurt you, I'm sorry."

Charlie appears spiritual and has an uncanny ability to sense people's moods and anticipate their actions. He will prevent a confrontation by solving the issue: withheld information suddenly becomes available, a lost item is suddenly found, a perceived breach is suddenly healed. Of course, he expects public appreciation as the "hero" in these situations. Ultimately, he uses people and worships control. He will use whatever means necessary to acquire and keep power—seduction, manipulation, intimidation, or domination.

Charlie is a little world to himself, bounded on the north, south, east, and west by "Charlie." For Charlie, *it is all about me*. His mantra is, "I matter; nobody else does."

This spirit seeps down into the root system and ultimately destroys relationships. It can turn a marriage into a living hell. It can tear families apart and make the workplace unbearable. It is typically the reason why churches split. This is a spirit from the pit of hell itself, ultimately seeking to block, or even destroy, our connection to God.

## Healing the Orphans of the Church

Author Stephen Mansfield asked Derek Prince how he felt about the Charismatic renewal when he first came to America. He responded by saying:

> It was like watching a child playing with adult toys. Rather than seeing the outpouring of the Spirit as a call to maturity, to the person of Jesus, people leaned toward the thrills and the experience of revival. People gathered around dynamic personalities whether they had any depth or not. The movement was fragmented, and no one could speak for the whole. It was tragic because God was doing powerful things in the lives of many, and there would have been much more had there been unity.

Mansfield then asked Derek Prince if that was the motivation behind the founding of the "Discipleship Movement?"

> Yes. We wanted to bring unity and order, hopefully of a kind that would lead to maturity. I must say that I believe that God ordained the Discipleship Movement, but that the response of some people to it was very carnal. It was right in its original motivation, though. Ultimately, selfish ambition destroyed it.

"Even your own selfish ambition?" asked Mansfield.

"Yes, I am sad to say."

The "we" Derek Prince mentions initially comprised a group of four men, later five:

Derek Prince, Don Basham, Bob Mumford, Charles Simpson, and later Ern Baxter.

The "Fab Four"—later "Five"—together founded the "Shepherding Movement," also known as the Discipleship Movement.

It did some good initially, but would ultimately destroy many lives. It became one of the most damaging controversies in American Christianity. The doctrine that every believer needed a personal pastor was central to their teaching. In March 1975 at a historic conference in Atlanta, the "Fab Five," assembled the men whom they pastored directly. The doctrines of the Shepherding Movement—greater accountability, strong character, development, and covenant relationships—were "imparted to their souls." Men signed written covenants of commitment to their pastors and took communion "not only as a remembrance of Jesus, but also as a sacrament of devotion to their human shepherds," says Mansfield.

Eventually, a chain-of-command structure emerged. It was shaped like a pyramid with the "Fab Five" at the top, of course. They insisted they were in mutual submission to each other. In its heyday, they had constructed a national network of followers who formed "pyramids of sheep and shepherds. Down through the pyramid went the orders, it was alleged, while up the same pyramid went the tithes." Many people moved their families to Fort Lauderdale—the movement's headquarters—so they could live the life described to them by their leaders.

Derek Prince would later say, "We each were filled with blind ambition (pride) and did not realize, until too late, the damage we had done. I wanted to be a popular and recognized Bible teacher!"

George Barna's book, *Revolution: Worn Out On the Church? Finding Vibrant Faith Beyond the Walls of the Sanctuary*, poses a question: "If the local church is God's answer to our spiritual needs, then why are most churched Christians so spiritually immature and desperate?"[27]

My "qualified" answer to that question is that orphans rule the church. We teach what we know, but we reproduce who we are. The church has become an orphan factory.

Barna describes the "hallmark" of this age as the "*busyness*" of people's lives. This is the quintessential orphan trait—*overextension*. Most people are busy medicating their spiritual uneasiness with religious and other activities. Barna also astutely observes the younger generation values personal authenticity over performance, which partly explains the decline in overall church growth.

Remember, orphans seek connection as a means of finding safety through control. So in a typical church, there is fellowship without intimacy, chatter without communion, and communication without connection. These dynamics explain the disconnect between what believers are called to be (salt and light), versus the current state of churched Christians.

Barna's research consistently shows:

- Eight out of ten believers do not experience God's presence during worship.
- They worship God only in church.
- Half of all believers have not felt connected to God for a year.

*On Spiritual Conversations*

- Most believers will not lead one soul to Christ during their lifetimes.
- Most do not specifically pray for the salvation of others.

*On Spiritual Growth*

- Fewer than ten percent of believers have a biblical worldview.

- Most believers spend more time watching TV than reading the Bible.
- Success for most believers is represented by wealth, vocational or family achievements, and physical well-being, not spiritual growth.

## On Serving

- Only twenty-five percent of believers consistently help those outside of their congregations.
- Most would rather give a donation to an organization than personally help a stranger in need.

## On Money

- Believers give an average of three percent of their income each year and are pleased with their "sacrificial" giving.
- Thirty-five percent claim to faithfully tithe (give ten percent), but fewer than ten percent do.

## On Friendships

- Fewer than twenty percent of believers have a deep mutually-accountable relationship.
- Most believers take their life cues from the media, the law, or family members, not from the Bible or sermons.

## On Family Faith

- Parents rely on the church to form their children spiritually.
- Fewer than ten percent of families worship together outside of church.
- The divorce rate among born-again believers is the same as for non-believers.

I concur with George Barna's findings to a large degree. However, we end up in slightly different places. My ministry as a counselor over the past twenty-five years bears witness to the shift (revolution) that Barna poignantly describes. Many mature believers (those who have gotten a revelation of God's love) are tired of the religious games and the proliferation of impressive clouds with no rain. They are sick of personality cults masquerading as churches. They lament the absence of genuine love and true fellowship in most of our churches.

However, I do not believe the answer is to abandon the current structure of church. I share Barna's admonition that we should be wise and discerning, but not judgmental. We cannot on one hand criticize the church for shooting its wounded, and then turn around and shoot its leaders. We end up in the same place.

Galatians 6:2 (NIV) says, "Carry each other's burdens, and in this way you will fulfill the law of Christ." In the spirit of Christ we must facilitate the healing of the orphans—those not yet obsessed with *love* being fully formed in them. Those of us who are already pursuing a deeper revelation of God's love owe our brethren love. We must stay in the arena and intercede, and allow God to use us as templates upon which His love is shed abroad to everyone in our sphere of influence and beyond.

# Oppression: The Invisible Taskmaster

> Also a multitude gathered from the surrounding cities
> to Jerusalem, bringing sick people and those who were
> tormented by unclean spirits, and they were all healed.
>
> (Acts 5:16 NKJV)

In researching missing children, I learned that a large percentage of missing children are those who, for one reason or another, did not feel at home in their homes, and became runaways. They are spiritual orphans who find themselves swallowed up in deeper waters than they ever imagined after running away.

This concept is oddly true for adults with orphan spirits who keep running away from deep hurt and disappointments, and who look for meaning and validation in temporal things. Orphans, such as our friend Jay in the first chapter. Jay was a pastor who devoted his life to bringing the gospel, the good news of healing, salvation, and hope in Christ, yet could not assimilate those truths into his own life and find comfort.

Heartbreak within the life cycle can often create a paradigm of pity for and within the "victim." Anyone who hears a story of child abuse cannot help feeling sorry for that child, and rightfully so. Such trauma has staggering emotional and psychological effects. However, as dire as those effects are, they are not the most important element of concern when it comes to properly assessing trauma and healing.

Important factors are our sin nature and whether we have allowed the finished work of the cross to be applied to our lives. Our sin nature will automatically encourage the wrong response to pain and heartbreak, and that response almost always turns us away from God. Proverbs 16:25 (NKJV) warns: "There is a way that seems right to a man, but its end is the way of death."

This truth is magnified in moments of pain and hurt. Our fallen nature responds well to the bidding of the enemy, and we move from just being hurt, to now sinning in our pain. Ephesians 4:26 warns us that though we can be angry, we must take care not to sin in our anger. Trauma creates a climate rife for sin. The list goes on: the sins of bitterness, unforgiveness, resentment, pride, and entitlement. All these are magnets for demonic oppression.

The enemy is attracted to orphans because they often battle with some of the above sin issues. They have the spiritual dynamics that make it easy for Satan to move in with lies that fuel self-hate, self-rejection, fear, addiction and much more.

Again, I repeat, love is a fundamental need of the soul. God created us out of love, for love. If we close ourselves off to love, a need remains, creating a void. Ephesians 4:27 tells us not to "give place" to the enemy. This void that orphans carry around is a very deep place in which the enemy can truly establish a stronghold. Because Christians with this worldview preach one thing but don't believe it for themselves, they open the door to deception, and the situation goes from bad to worse.

We have an adversary roaming about seeking whom he may devour, and he has an arsenal of weapons to use against us. Let's discuss two of those weapons: *oppression* and *invasion*. Merriam-Webster's Dictionary defines "oppress" as: *to burden with cruel or unjust impositions or restraints; subject to a burdensome or harsh exercise of authority or power.*

The children of Israel were oppressed in Egypt.

> Therefore they set taskmasters over them to afflict them with their burdens. And they built for Pharaoh supply cities, Pithom and Raamses. But the more they afflicted them, the more they multiplied and grew. And they were in dread of the children of Israel. So the Egyptians made the children of Israel serve with rigor. And they made their lives bitter with hard bondage—in mortar, in brick, and in all manner of service in the field. All their service in which they made them serve was with rigor.
>
> (Ex. 1:11-14 NKJV)

Spiritual oppression is like having an invisible taskmaster.

> For we do not wrestle against flesh and blood, but against principalities, against powers, against the rulers of the darkness of this age, against spiritual hosts of wickedness in the heavenly places.
>
> (Eph. 6:12 NKJV)

It is likely that our friend Jay had oppressive forces pushing him over the edge, reaffirming the lie that he was not loved, and could not be understood, and must stay locked away behind walls of fear and dread.

Prior to taking his own life in his home, actor and comedian Robin Williams relayed to those closest to him he could no longer stand the voices, nor the torment and the oppression of his soul.

Often what sounds like our own voice is in fact the enemy's voice in disguise. This reinforces misbeliefs we hold and lies we have been told, overwhelming our souls with oppressive emotions. Here anger escalates to rage, foreboding to gripping fear, and avoidance to outright denial. Every negative emotion is magnified to have its greatest impact.

Derek Prince, having worked with countless victims of oppression, explained these spiritual forces compel, tempt, torment and drive people beyond their limits.

David aptly captured the torment of his enemies:

> He sent from above, He took me;
> He drew me out of many waters.
> He delivered me from my strong enemy,
> From those who hated me,
> For they were too strong for me.
> They confronted me in the day of my calamity,
> But the LORD was my support.
> (Ps. 18:16-18 NKJV)

Oppression is not fun. It cannot be shaken by mere will power. The enemy relentlessly uses persuasive powers of suggestion to enslave his victims. Orphans who are not anchored in truth often fall prey. The oppression may come in seasons. There are some who battle depression only during the holidays or during the month when a loved one passed away. God does not want us caught in a cycle of seasonal oppression. "So if the Son sets you free, you will be free indeed" (John 8:36 NIV).

The nature of any given oppression does not necessarily have to drive its victim to suicide. Oppression is tailor-made for its victim. The enemy will torment with whatever vice a person is most responsive to. Some people are driven by greed, obsession, insecurity, competition; the list goes on. There are many forms of oppression, but the goal is always the same: to kill, steal and destroy. Oppression saps virtue and truth from its victim.

I met with an older gentleman for brief counseling session. He had recently rededicated his life to the Lord. All was great, and he was ecstatic about his experience with God, except for one thing. "Everything is going well except for when that lust comes on me. I can't shake it. It's as if I have to do its bidding. I've got to get rid of this thing."

As we conversed, the Lord made it clear he was battling an oppressive spirit of lust. The answer was deliverance. Oppression breaks when it is confronted. It does not lift just through repentance. Repentance gets you back in proper fellowship with God; it does not directly address your enemies.

A young lady who came to me for help was like the many drifters and homeless individuals I have seen who talk to themselves and behave erratically as if some unseen person were following them and having a conversation with them. She heard a message about oppression and came because she too was at the point of giving up. Holding a bottle of pills in her hand she explained: "I was going to take these, but now I know I'm not crazy. Someone understands . . . Until now I couldn't talk to anyone about the fear that overwhelms me; makes me want to run into the streets and kill myself. I couldn't tell anyone about the voices that tell me I'm a failure and I'm better off dead. They keep reminding me of my past."

When she heard the message about oppression and how Jesus truly came to set captives free, she asked for prayer and counseling. Today she is stable and anchored. In counseling this woman, I had to explain to her the power of God can drive her enemies away, however, if she continued to resist the love of the Father, her enemies would soon return. God is greater than any oppressive force. However, the Holy Spirit must occupy the place given to the enemy, or the individual will return to that place of fear and dread.

One night at about 11 p.m., I got a call from one my counselees complaining he could not sleep. "I'm uneasy, and afraid to fall asleep."

"Did something happen? Did you hear a noise? Was it something outside?"

He responded, "No," to all of my inquiries.

I sensed a spirit of fear was oppressing him. "You first need to repent for any open door in your life," I told him. "Then speak specifically over your room this verse: 'For God has not given us a spirit of fear, but of power and of love and of a sound mind'" Besides 2 Timothy 1:7 (NKJV), I gave him some other passages to say aloud. Before long the atmosphere in his room had completely changed.

The enemy is an oppressor! He's a bully. Jesus came to heal all those who were oppressed of the devil. Oppression often requires healing. The healing is for those wounds that opened the door to the enemy in the first place. After the enemy is exposed and expelled, healing must be received.

Invasion is another arsenal the enemy loves to use even on Christians. Jesus came to set the captives free. Many of those captives are believers. We assume because we are believers we are free from the invasion of the enemy. Hosea 4:6 says, "My people perish from lack of knowledge."

Most of the church focuses on knowing Jesus and the blessings bestowed on us. However, we are warned not to be ignorant of the enemy's devices (2 Cor. 2:11). We know we have an enemy, but few understand his methods, and his inroads. He is an enemy who loves to attack those with an orphan mentality, who are insecure in God's love for them.

Only in Christianity do we mistake working for God with knowing him. In our secular lives, it is easily understood we won't necessarily have a personal relationship with the CEO, just because we work for an organization. Orphans often equate knowing God with *doing* for God.

There will be many on judgment day who will hear, after they have listed all they have *done* for the Lord, "I never knew you," to their shock and dismay. "There was no communion. We are not friends. You never let me in."

Herein lies the key to true salvation of the soul: *communion*. "Where the Spirit of the Lord is, there is liberty" (2 Cor. 3:17 NKJV). There is freedom—but we must let the Spirit in!

When we come to God for healing we must put our guard down. We are safe with him. If we dissociate from our circumstances, our problems or hurts, we will come in and out of his presence unchanged and in a form of pretense. Compartmentalizing problems and issues creates a perfect door for the enemy. Each compartment can be fed a set of lies; invasive spirits move from merely oppressing to *occupying*. We humans do not do well with voids and vacuums. They are magnets for evil spirits.

When we as believers declare to others that Jesus is a healer, yet we ourselves go through life with open wounds and unresolved issues—even if they are repressed in our subconscious—we become easy targets for the enemy. We are considered hypocritical. We will preach the good news to others, but won't take the medicine ourselves. An even greater resentment is created within us when we look around and find others walking in healing, yet we remain emotionally and spiritually stuck in a trauma that happened many years ago.

One Sunday, the Lord impressed upon me to teach on overcoming rejection. An altar call was made for those who had experienced various forms of rejection. The altar was filled with wounded souls who did not know how to trust, to receive or give love; it was full of orphans. As I began to pray and lay hands on these precious people, many began to cough and convulse as the Holy Spirit drove out the invasive forces that lived within them, occupying voids created by a need for love. Some had spirits of inadequacy, others of hatred, lust, secrets, religion, anger; the list seemed endless. If we are going to embark on a path of healing, freedom from oppressive forces must be part of our process. The enemy will not go unless he is commanded to do so.

# Finding True Freedom

The Spirit of the Lord GOD is upon Me,
Because the LORD has anointed Me
To preach good tidings to the poor;
He has sent Me to heal the brokenhearted,
To proclaim liberty to the captives,
And the opening of the prison to those who are bound;
To proclaim the acceptable year of the LORD
And the day of vengeance of our God;
To comfort all who mourn,
To console those who mourn in Zion,
To give them beauty for ashes, the oil of joy for mourning,
The garment of praise for the spirit of heaviness;
That they may be called trees of righteousness,
The planting of the Lord, that He may be glorified.

(Isa. 61:1-3 NKJV)

S o many in the church today are battling but do not
know what or why they are battling. That is why truth
is so essential. Scripture tells us "the truth will set you
free" (John 8:32 NIV).

The truth is both the person of Jesus Christ and his Word! In *Hurt People Hurt People: Hope and Healing for Yourself and Your Relationships*, Sandra D. Wilson writes, "Truth brings suffering as well as freedom. Increased hurting before increased health."[28]

Freedom demands we abandon all destructive coping mechanisms, renew our minds and release hurts that have shaped our identity.

Recently, at a conference in Huntsville, Alabama, I had the privilege of hearing the remarkable journey of Bob and Audrey Meisner. I sat a couple of rows behind this attractive couple, not knowing who they were. They were fully engaged with each other and seemed to display genuine respect and affection for each other.

Audrey spoke first. In an excruciatingly transparent style she told the story of her betrayal of Bob and her journey to redemption and purpose. She came from a deeply devout family and gave her life to Christ at an early age. She and Bob had met and married in Bible school. They eventually founded a church, and had three children, were active in their community, and were loved and respected.

Bob said, after seventeen years together, he felt comfortable in his role as husband, father and TV personality. He thought they had a great marriage.

However, things were different for Audrey. She'd been feeling "unheard" and not cherished for a long time.

As is often the case with pastors, they were drawn to a wounded young man who had no family and invited him into their family circle. Over time, he took advantage of the "dryness" in Audrey's soul, began lavishing her with attention that eventually led to a sexual affair.

After three weeks, Audrey felt convicted, severed the relationship and confessed to her husband Bob.

The initial shock had not even settled in when they discovered Audrey was pregnant. Bob had had a vasectomy so she was carrying another man's baby. And oh—the baby was biracial!

In a deeply moving presentation Bob shared about the sweeping anger and despair that nearly consumed him. Yet, while in the throes of his pain, he purposed in his heart to cover his wife and stay in the marriage. Remarkably, he not only accepted the child, but also named him after himself—Robert Theodore Meisner. Theodore means "God's gift!" Wow!

The pain and shame did not disappear after Robert was born. Audrey shared about the shame, rejection, and pain that stalked them for the first few years after the affair. However, she continued to allow God to "meet her" in her broken places until the day she was joyously baptized in God's love. The shame fell away and the unshakeable knowledge that she was loved beyond her actions flooded her soul with joy that she exudes even today.

Bob was candid about his jealously over her newfound freedom in Christ. However, he used it as fuel to surrender to God's love also. Bob and Audrey could have stayed stuck in a cycle of recrimination and justification. They could have continued practicing the presence of shame and anger. Instead they chose to contend for love as well as an anointed ministry. Today the Meisners live in Arizona where they host a TV ministry that is beamed into Canada, and they conduct marriage retreats around the world.

The Meisners' story touched me deeply and renewed my confidence in God's power and desire to heal broken hearts. Thank God for that reminder. I returned home to news that a high-impact ministry couple had decided to get a divorce. The wife insisted her husband agree to a public shaming for an affair he had confessed to years before. When he refused, she filed for divorce. The divorce was bitter and acrimonious. Today she wishes she had made a different choice. Deep, unhealed wounds that preceded the marriage had blinded her. She had watched her mother put up with her father's serial infidelity. Over the years she watched the light go out of her mother's eyes as she began to wear her heartache on her face. So, she had made a vow she would never live like her mom. One breech was too much. Today, with God's grace, she is allowing God to heal her heart and reconnect her to her family.

This situation is not that uncommon. I pray God will open our eyes to see our own needs and the needs of the people around us. We can always use more forgiveness and reconciliation.

Let's take a look at what the kind of healing Bob and Audrey experienced looks like.

## Healing is (but is not limited to):

- A journey into an infinite God, not a destination
- More than the absence of orphan traits, it is an all-consuming desire to receive and be animated by God's love and then offering that love to "whosoever."
- Being more and more connected to all human beings; actually to all of God's creation
- The capacity to live beyond ego
- Seeking to be the least to the most and the most to the "least of these"

- Moving beyond connecting to oneness with God
- A wish desired and a wish fulfilled melding together
- Communion
- Abandonment to divine providence
- Progressive detachment from outcomes
- A craving to transmit God's thoughts and feelings to the world
- A burning desire to sacrifice comfort so others can find God
- Living free of judgment for God, self, and others
- Being graced with the ability and willingness to forgive and release offense
- Walking in forgiveness
- Enthusiasm about spending time with Abba
- Ministering and living from a position of rest
- A palpable desire to do God's will, not our own.

I beseech you therefore, brethren, by the mercies of God, that you present your bodies a living sacrifice, holy, acceptable to God, which is your reasonable service.

(Rom. 12:1 NKJV)

By now, dear reader, you have no doubt found common cause with one or more characters profiled in this book. The things that threaten one member threaten all of us, for we are all members of one body. Ultimately, I invite you to be willing to step out of your comfort zone (grave) and contend for love. I offer this roadmap as a guide.

1. **Consecration.**
   I often say, "Nothing can be resolved until it is confronted." We must start by setting some time aside to be real with God and ourselves. God is relentlessly calling us back to himself. However, we have to

intentionally unyoke ourselves from all the idols we use to medicate our pain in order to hear his voice and answer the call.

In Psalm 46:10 we are exhorted to be "still" so we can know God and exalt him above all. In Hosea 2:14-15, God draws unfaithful Gomer (a picture of Israel) into the wilderness so he can speak comfort to her. He also promised to give her vineyards back to her and turn the Valley of Achor (a place of shame and death) into a door of hope. God wants us to voluntarily give ourselves back to him solely as a response to his love and faithfulness. He wants us to trust him with all of our heart, soul, strength, as well as our mind. He wants us to give ourselves totally to him and trust that he has a hope and an expected (good) end for us. We are his by "right," but he wants us to desire to be his by choice.

2. **We Must Own Our Issues.**
   Healing requires we acknowledge our participation in the breach. We are either perpetrators or reactive victims who disconnected or lashed out in return. We must commit ourselves to become stewards of connection again. Bitterness, unforgiveness, revenge, withdrawal of affection, active or passive wickedness, vicious backbiting, etc., are all symptoms of disconnection from the bond of love. When we fail to discern the body of Christ (the church), we choose to forgo vital, life-giving fellowship in exchange for alienation and morbidity. This invariably leads to death even before we die. This is where diseases of the spirit, soul and body are conceived. When we approach the Lord with lowliness of heart and contrition, he promises to lavish us with his grace and the power to overcome all the ravages of sin.

3. **We All Need Safe Places.**

We need places where we can unburden ourselves without judgment or fear of rejection. Sin, whether perpetrated or absorbed, tends to distort our image of God, self and others. Often we need the clear vision of an anointed counselor, coach, guide, soul-friend (one who does not depend on his intellect and training alone, but is led by God's Spirit). This is one not jaded by our narrative of misery and self-justification who can guide us back into full fellowship with God and man. Jesus, our creator, understood this essential truth when he promised never to leave us or forsake us. That is why he sent us the gift of the Holy Spirit (John 14) to guide us into all truth. That truth and that sweet, rejuvenating Spirit is best mediated by yielded vessels—anointed counselors, coaches, soul-friends and fellow travelers in this journey. It also offers us a platform to sow humility and accountability as well as an opportunity to trust again. The many "one anothers" of Scripture (Gal. 6:1-2, John 13:34-35, James 5:16, etc.) highlight the necessity for connection in perfect love to God, self and then others.

4. **Talk it Out.**

We must give voice to our pain and replace the narrative of affliction with the narrative of redemption. "Be transformed by the renewing of your mind" (Rom. 12:2 NKJV). Too often we make lies our refuge and hide ourselves under false banners of self-preservation and autonomy, thereby making a covenant with hell (Isa. 28:15). We must replace the narrative of the grave with the narrative of Christ and his redeeming power. Shine a light where darkness has ruled and darkness must disappear. Find an anointed and tested counselor/ confessor and talk it out.

5.  **Forgive.**
    Earnestly desire to forgive those who have hurt you. The Lord commands us to forgive. That means the grace is available, but we have to be willing for that grace to be activated. It may not be instant, but it will come. Purpose in your heart to forgive all the people who have hurt you. It does not mean you condone what they did. It means you trust in the justice of God. It might require fasting and prayer. (It is prudent to consult with your doctor before fasting if you have health issues.)

6.  **Cultivate the Mind of Christ.**
    We need new minds. We must seek to cultivate the mind of Christ. Memorize Scriptures that reveal God's character and intention towards you. Be diligent in studying and meditating on the Scriptures that remind you of your identity as a child of the Most High God. He knows you by name. He has an inheritance for you that is totally unaffected by what's been done to you or how you reacted to it in the past. Those things are now passed away. Your desire now is to live, to move, and have your being in Christ alone.

7.  **Devote Yourself to the Way of Love.**
    It starts by making an intentional choice to stay connected to God and the brethren, come hell or high water! The way of love requires a dogged commitment to cultivate the attributes of love as in 1 Corinthians 13—kindness, patience, humility, temperance, mercy, trust, longsuffering, and especially the discipline to refrain from rejoicing in iniquity. We must never distort

Scripture to justify our ends, no matter the hurt. When we make the choice to present ourselves as living sacrifices, God promises to meet us there and take us the rest of the way. Love will turn us around and point us back to God every time.

Frank, tall, lean, and handsome, makes a grand entrance everywhere he goes—including my office. Dressed to the nines, he accentuated his look with a pink headband draped around his graying locks.

"Go ahead; lay it on me," he said. "I've been taking it my whole life."

"Lay what on you?" I asked as I followed his lead and sat on the floor across from him. This gentle soul went on to tell me about his life.

Frank was placed in the Corsicana State Home for Orphans in the early fifties. He was the target of abuse right from the start because he was "cute and fragile." He was taunted, hit, and harassed constantly by both students and supervisors alike. Worse yet, some "clergy" began taking him home on weekends where he was repeatedly molested.

"How did you survive such horror, Frank?"

"Well, God placed Miss Mable in my life."

Mable was a black cleaning lady who took Frank under her wing. She would tell him, "Frank, ask God to forgive them, child. They don't know what they be doin.' Be like Stephen."

"I would say that all the time," Frank said. I still say it today."

"That's wisdom." I nodded. "So Frank, why are you here today?"

"Well, I read the obituary of my worst abuser yesterday. People said nice things about him. It made me really angry. So I'm here to confess to you that I forgive him and hold no bitterness in my heart."

Shattering all stereotypes, Frank has been happily married for over thirty years to the same lady he calls his angel. Frank knows the power of forgiveness and it has set him free.

"The Lord is close to the brokenhearted and saves those who are crushed in spirit," (Ps. 34:18 NIV).

An article on today.com by Rebecca Ruiz (September 19, 2013) shows the potency of devoting yourself to the power of love.

Mary Johnson suffered a devastating loss in February 1993 when her twenty-year-old son, and only child, Laramiun Byrd, was shot to death after an argument at a party. His killer was a sixteen year old named Oshea Israel. Oshea was tried as an adult and sentenced to twenty-five and one-half years in prison.

At the time of the trial, Mary told Oshea she had forgiven him. However, it took years of travail and prayer for the word "forgiveness" to feel true in Mary's heart. She eventually felt compelled to visit him in prison. Johnson describes her experience as she hugged Oshea Israel for the first time.

Afterwards she "doubled over in shock" saying over and over, "I just hugged the man who killed my son."

"I felt something leave me," she said. "Instantly I knew all the hatred, bitterness and animosity—I knew it was gone."

Mary followed that visit with many others over the years. When Oshea was freed after seventeen years and returned to his old neighborhood, Mary Johnson lobbied her landlord to rent Oshea an apartment close to her. In fact, right next door to her. The two have become very close. Mary calls him her spiritual son, and he calls her his second mom.

Oshea has since found a job, working during the day and attending college at night. The two share their experience of forgiveness through Mary's ministry, From Death to Life, that promotes healing and reconciliation between the families of victims and those who caused them harm.

Mary Johnson isn't condoning what Israel did to her son, but she did it to rid herself of her own suffering. "All that stuff had to leave me," she said. "And the day I went to prison, I was delivered."

# The "Beat" of Redemptive Love

## The Rasa Testimony

Looking at Michael and Debbie Rasa today, it is nearly impossible to imagine the brokenness they came out of.

Michael was raised in a broken home. His father was physically and verbally abusive. As a little boy he yearned to be free, yet was afraid of freedom. This tension eventually created an obsessive need to control his environment and protect his heart. He was kicked out of his home at fourteen, shortly before his parents got divorced. He joined the army at eighteen where he cultivated discipline and a strong work ethic. Eventually, he reconnected with his older brother and was inspired by the open displays of affection among members of his brother's family. Upon leaving the army, he married, and the couple had two children. However, Michael's drive to prove himself worthy of love caused him to strive for perfection in everything—a futile effort indeed.

Debbie did not know her father growing up. Her mom remarried several times so she learned to be self-reliant and self-sufficient at a very young age. She developed a very strong work ethic early. "You work hard, you bury your feelings and emotions and 'dry it up!'" In her world back then, there was no time to cry or feel much of anything.

By the time she was fourteen, she had lost her beloved grandmother to suicide and her six-year-old cousin was hit and killed by a car. However, the most excruciating childhood loss was that of Mel, her Sunday school teacher.

When she was twelve, she and her very best friend Kay had "stumbled" upon a church and decided to attend Sunday school together. Mel took them under his wing and sowed God's love and character into their hearts. When he died, church, God, and faith all "died" for Debbie as she focused on survival. What Mel had planted would be awakened again some twenty-five years later when Debbie was in her forties.

After high school, Debbie married her sweetheart and tried to settle down. When her husband was convicted of a crime and sent to prison a year later, she moved to another state to get a fresh start. She got a job as a waitress/bartender and worked very long hours. Not long thereafter, her best friend committed suicide. She coped with all the devastating losses by building walls around her heart and making a vow never to hurt or feel the devastation ever again. Debbie began to medicate her pain with work, alcohol and relationships. She was determined to work her way to the top. Soon her identity became inextricably linked to her performance at work.

Debbie married again and had a daughter but continued the cycle of work, more work, alcohol, and eventually another affair.

Debbie met Michael on Valentine's Day 1995. When they met, both were still married. He had two daughters; she had one. Michael started a company in 1994, and Debbie met and joined him seven months later. They eventually divorced their spouses and married each other, leaving in their wake some devastating collateral damage. About one year into their marriage, the shame, guilt, and gut-wrenching judgments they had heaped upon each other came crashing down upon them.

In 1999, Michael and Debbie met Jesus and fell in love with him. They got into biblical counseling shortly thereafter and embraced God's blueprint for their marriage, their family, and their business.

"Suddenly everything was different for us and in our lives," says Debbie. "We were baptized together, along with one of our daughters, in 2001. From that point forward, nothing would ever look, feel or be the same."

Their three beautiful girls are now twenty-eight, twenty-seven, and twenty-five and are all devoted followers of Jesus Christ. The two older daughters are married to godly men and the youngest is in a committed relationship. So far there is one grandson, with another on the way. All three girls are also successful career women. One is a graphic designer, the other a marriage and family counselor, and the youngest is well on her way to becoming a registered dietitian.

The company that Michael and Debbie started in 1994 now employs about one hundred and forty people with over three hundred subcontractors. They have ten stores in three states—Texas, Oklahoma, and Louisiana. Their entire company is guided by and infused with God's love. Each store has a staff chaplain entrusted with the spiritual and personal well-being of their co-workers and families.

Michael and Debbie have a fabulous relationship today. They firmly believe this is primarily because they allowed God's love to redeem their past. They purposed in their hearts to love God back with all of them—their hearts, souls, strength, and minds (see Luke 10:27). They are passionate about sharing that redemptive love with the entire world.

Michael and Debbie Rasa say, "Happiness is fleeting, but true, deep-down joy is something only God can give. We will do everything in our power to be obedient and honor God in all things from our personal lives to our workplace, and even our resources, to build up the kingdom and be wrung out for him and his purposes. We can't even explain how grateful and blessed we feel today to have gone through this amazing transformation through the redemptive power of God's great love! We are humbled indeed."

Dear friend, this could be your testimony too!

## My Own Story

In an earlier chapter I briefly described my "diem horribilis" several months after my wife Alexandria died. It seems fitting as I close to share some details about my testimony of presumption, acute pain, and loss, then redemptive love that is still ushering me home even today.

On August 15, 2007 my wife, Alexandria, died suddenly. We had been married for just over a year at that point. To compound the situation, I was in the Caribbean when it happened. My family withheld the news from me until the next day. Due to an impending storm, it took me a couple of days to make it back to Dallas. Alone in a hotel room with the storm gathering outside, I alternated between fits of crying, numbness, and deep anguish. I wept, too, for my 14-year-old daughter's perpetual heartbreak. And, yes, there was anger at God.

The familiar, resplendent and deeply satisfying symphony with its alluring chimes and reverberating base tones that cushioned life and made it really enjoyable for the past year, had suddenly fallen silent. Left in its wake was acute nostalgia and what, at that point, sounded to me like an unrelenting, "infernal" beat. What do you do when the music stops but the beat goes on?

As I look back now, that beat—often unrecognized—is the persistent call of God to return *home* to his *love*. It's what the poet Francis Thompson describes as "The Hound of Heaven," the love that pursues us even into "hell," or the end of the earth; a love that is always there because "Naught shelters thee, who will not shelter me." As C.S. Lewis reminds us, "Hell is the greatest monument to human freedom."[29] We can choose to either accept or reject this love. I chose not only to reject this love, but made a convincing case against it in my own mind and woke up one day in my own "hell."

The beat had always been there to comfort, remind, encourage, warn, convict, and if necessary "wound." Ultimately, it is there to guide me back home to God's love. I had taken it for granted; even labeled it as infernal and eventually drowned it out by the noise of my complaint and willful presumptions.

After love rescued me, I made two determinations that transformed that beat into the sound of grace, that same amazing grace that continues to lead me home—deeper into the limitless love of Abba Father.

One: *God is good—all the time*. I have settled the issue in my heart. I have unflinching confidence in the character of God and his good intentions toward me today and forever.

Two: *I do not know what is ultimately good or evil*. So I leave all judgments of God, others, or myself to God. I trust his leading in all things. Oh what a relief it is to live without judgment! Bitter things are made sweet and burdens become truly light.

God's love for us never waivers. That love also speaks. Call it instinct, intuition, discernment, inner beckoning, inner knowing, that "something" as in "something told me," is always there, drawing, pulling, calling, leading us home.

Following that beat led me to seasons of deep satisfaction that I had mislabeled as the fruit of my own goodness/diligence. What self-righteousness! Interestingly, the beat was faintest during times that were replete with indulgences that blinded me—ergo the trap of the prosperity gospel.

The beat was always crisper and clearer during the seasons I chose the path infused with the obligations that awaken. If you trust this beat, you may be maligned and misconstrued by even those closest to you. Your decisions will often be at odds with common sense and self-preservation. However, if we are willing and obedient, that beat, animated by grace, will lead us home to God's love—heaven on earth.

That beat calls us to practice patience, kindness, perseverance, humility, gentleness, generosity of spirit, and good neighborliness with each other. Animated by grace, we are constantly invited to choreograph these qualities into our lives just as the apostle Peter reminds us (2 Peter 1:3-9 NIV).

> His divine power has given us everything we need for life and godliness through our knowledge of him who called us by his own glory and goodness. Through these he has given us his very great and precious promises, so that through them you may participate in the divine nature and escape the corruption in the world caused by evil desires. For this very reason, make every effort to add to your faith goodness; and to goodness, knowledge; and

to knowledge, self-control; and to self-control, perseverance; and to perseverance, godliness; and to godliness,
brotherly kindness; and to brotherly kindness, love. For
if you possess these qualities in increasing measure, they
will keep you from being ineffective and unproductive in
your knowledge of our Lord Jesus Christ. But if anyone
does not have them, he is near-sighted and blind, and has
forgotten that he has been cleansed from his past sins.

We also do not rejoice in iniquity. Do we reject any
thought or action directed at ourselves or others, that
distorts the truth that we are all precious in God's sight?
That is one of the greatest buffers against bitterness and
unforgiveness. We can learn to bear each other's burdens,
thus fulfilling the law of Christ—which is love (Gal. 6:2).

Thus, God's love is no longer refracted in our hearts and
aimed at faults—my faults or the faults of others. Judgment
is thus ruthlessly rooted out and replaced by understanding
and solidarity even as we maintain appropriate boundaries
with our fellow human beings.

Instead, God's love is now reflected or shed abroad in
our hearts by the Holy Spirit. This kind of love does not seek
its own. It does not point the finger of judgment, nor keep
a record of wrongs. Instead, it covers (protects) a multitude
of sins and always intercedes for others.

My wife Alexandria's death exposed, and then punched a
gaping hole in my erstwhile childish kind of love that 1 Cor.
13:11 tells us we should put away. Until then, like Micah
in the Old Testament, I kept my idols, paid my "priest"
(pastor), so "the Lord will do me good" (Judges 17:13 KJV).
Ten shekels of silver, designer suits, and a good living—that
is utilitarian religion to the core!

So when that fateful phone call came, that "good" turned
into a nightmare of loss, pain, loneliness, and despair. My

love for God began to wax cold even as disappointment and anger with God burned hotter every day.

It is typically not the mountaintop experiences that facilitate the maturing of love. Rather, it is the Gethsemanes, and Golgothas, and the altars of betrayal (Peter—"I do not know this man"—denying Jesus!), that reveal the depth of selfishness and childish love within our hearts.

We can respond like Peter with deep sorrow and repentance that converts that love into mature, other-centered compassion. Or we can react like Judas, who could not get past himself, choosing instead to execute his own outcome.

The story of the rich young ruler (Luke 18:18-23) offers us some wonderful lessons about God's love. We can fulfill all the requirements of the Law and still miss the essential thing. Jesus loved that man but gave him the choice to receive or reject his love.

"This one thing you lack . . ."

This is a "come-to-Jesus moment," dear reader. As believers, we have placed our faith in Jesus, so our place in heaven is already settled. However, until then, what do you lack today? Is it peace, joy, assurance of salvation, the power to overcome a habit?

Then I invite you to enter into a deeply personal transaction between you and God. Stop and take inventory to identify what you are lacking. Peace, joy, acceptance, and ultimately love, are not things that can be achieved. They can only be received. Dr. Mary Neal, an orthopedic surgeon who died and was sent back to earth as a witness of God's love, described God's love as "intense, pure, and alluring."[30] Allow yourself to be wooed by God's love again.

However, we must be willing to give up our counterfeits in order to create room for the real. We must do so unreservedly without one plea:

# The "Beat" of Redemptive Love

Just as I am, without one plea
But that thy blood was shed for me,
And that thou bidst me come to Thee,
O Lamb of God, I come, I come.
(Charlotte Elliott 1835)

Amazing grace, how sweet the sound! The beat that remains is the sound of grace in our lives. You want to hear the sound of grace? Listen to your heartbeat, your breath, a baby's laughter. That grace empowers us to finally go back home into Abba's embrace.

Orphans no more! Welcome home.

# Endnotes

1.  Emmerich Vogt, *The Freedom to Love: Recovery and the Seven Deadly Sins* (Minneapolis: Mill City Press, 2012).

2.  John Dear and William Hart McNichols, *You Will Be My Witnesses: Saints, Prophets, and Martyrs* (Mary Knoll, New York: Orbis Books, 2006).

3.  Zachary Lester, *Afro Briefs*, November 12, 2013.

4.  Westminster Assembly, *Westminster Shorter Catechism* (1647).

5.  Aleksandr Solzhenitsyn, *The Gulag Archipelago, 1918-1956.*

6.  Nick Valencia, *CNN* report 8/23/2015.

7.  Frank Peretti, *The Wounded Spirit* (Nashville: Word Publishing, 2000).

8.  Bob Buford, *Halftime: Changing Your Game Plan From Success to Significance* (Grand Rapids: Zondervan, 2008).

9.  Stephen T. Sinatra, *Heartbreak and Heart Disease: A Mind/ Body Prescription for Healing the Heart* (New Canaan, CT: Keats Publishing, 1996).

10. Angela Saini, "Epigenetics: Genes, Environment and the Generation Game," *The Guardian*, September 6, 2014.

11. National Center for Victims of Crime, 2014.

12. C. S. Lewis, *The Four Loves: The Much Beloved Exploration of the Nature of Love* (Orlando: Harcourt, Inc., 1971).

13. Abraham Joshua Heschel, *I Asked for Wonder: A Spiritual Anthology* (NY: The Crossroad Publishing Co., 1983).

14. Fil Anderson, *Running on Empty: Contemplative Spirituality for Overachievers* (Colorado Springs: WaterBrook Press, 2004).

15. Tullian Tchividjian, "Ladder Christianity," Christianity. com blog, November 27, 2014.

16. Stephen Mansfield, *Derek Prince: A Biography* (Lake Mary, FL: Charisma House, 2005).

17. Rudyard Kipling, "If," *Rewards and Fairies*, 1910.

18. Warner Brothers, *The Judge*, 2014.

19. Stephen T. Sinatra, *Heartbreak and Heart Disease: A Mind/ Body Prescription for Healing the Heart* (New Canaan, CT: Keats Publishing, 1996), 35.

20. Daniel Coyle, *The Talent Code: Greatness Isn't Born* (NY: Bantam Books, 2009).

21. Martin Eisenstadt, Andre Haynal, Pierre Rentchnick, Pie De Denarclesn, *Parental Loss and Achievement* (Madison, Conn: International Universities Press, 1989).

22. HBO Films, *Tapia*, 2014, exec. producers, Curtis "50 Cent" Jackson, Lou Dibella, dir. Eddie Alcazar.

23. Dale Hansen, "Unplugged," WFAA, January 5, 2015, produced by ABC Broadcasting.

24. John and Paula Sandford, *The Elijah Task* (Lake Mary, FL: Charisma House, 2006).

25. Paul Tournier, *Escape From Loneliness* (Westminster: John Knox Press, 1977).

26. Stephen Mansfield, *Derek Prince: A Biography* (Lake Mary, FL: Charisma House, 2005).

27. Jack Frost, *Spiritual Slavery to Spiritual Sonship* (Shippensburg, PA: Destiny Image, 2006).

28. George Barna, *Revolution: Worn Out on the Church? Finding Vibrant Faith Beyond the Walls of the Sanctuary* (Carol Stream, Ill.: Tyndale House Publishing, 2012).

29. Sandra D. Wilson, *Hurt People, Hurt People* (Grand Rapids, MI: Discovery House, 2001).

30. C.S. Lewis, *The Problem of Pain* (NY City: Harper Collins 2009).

31. Mary Neal, *To Heaven and Back: A Doctor's Extraordinary Account of Her Death, Heaven, Angels, and Life Again* (Colorado Springs: Waterbrook Press, 2012).

# Contact Information

**REDEMPTION**
PRESS

To order additional copies of this book, please visit
www.redemption-press.com.
Also available on Amazon.com and BarnesandNoble.com
Or by calling toll free 1-844-2REDEEM
Also available through www.drnickeno.com

www.ingramcontent.com/pod-product-compliance
Lightning Source LLC
Chambersburg PA
CBHW050449290526
45786CB00006B/2225